BEHIND THE VEIL: REPRESENTATION OF MUSLIM WOMAN IN INDIAN WRITINGS IN ENGLISH 1950-2000

Edited by
A.R. Kidwai

A P H PUBLISHING CORPORATION
5 ANSARI ROAD, DARYA GANJ
NEW DELHI-110 002

Published by
S.B. Nangia
A P H Publishing Corporation
5 Ansari Road, Darya Ganj
New Delhi-110002
☎23274050
Email : aphbooks@vsnl.net

ISBN 81-313-0150-8

2007

Typesetting at
Paragon Computers
B-36, Chanakya Place
New Delhi-110 059
☎ 25509417

Printed at
Balaji offset
Navin Shahdara,Delhi-32
Ph:22324437

With gratitude

to

Professor Kapil Kapoor

Professor of English and concurrent Professor of Sanskrit
Jawaharlal Nehru University, New Delhi

Contents

Acknowledgements

- University Grants Commission, New Delhi, for awarding me the Major Research Project, "Representation of Muslim Woman in post-Independence Indian Writings in English (1950-2000)."
- Association of Commonwealth Universities / Commonwealth Commission/British Council/ University of Leicester, UK for awarding me Commonwealth Fellowship and Visiting Professorship.
- Professor Akhtar A.Siddiqui, Director, UGC ASC , Jamia Millia Islamia, New Delhi for granting the permission to reproduce Sabina Kidwai's piece which had originally appeared in the UGC ASC, Jamia Millia Islamia *Newsletter*.
- My alma mater and employer, Aligarh Muslim University, Aligarh for granting me leave.
- Professor A.A. Ansari, AMU, Aligarh, Professor Vincent Newey, Professor Gordon Campbell and Professor Richard Foulkes, Dept. of English, University of Leicester, UK for their encouragement and support.
- My colleagues for contributing articles to the Volume.
- Mr. M. Naved Khan and my son, Abdul Haleem Kidwai for their technical help.

A.R.Kidwai

Contributors

Masoodul Hasan, formerly Professor and Chairman, Department of English, Aligarh Muslim University, Aligarh

A.R.Kidwai, Professor, Department of English, Aligarh Muslim University; Commonwealth Fellow/Visiting Professor, Department of English, University of Leicester, UK

Md. Mahmudul Hasan, Ph.D. Student, Department of English, University of Portsmouth, UK

Seemin Hasan, Reader, Department of English, Aligarh Muslim University

Asim Siddiqui, Reader, Department of English, Aligarh Muslim University

Sami Rafiq, Lecturer, Department of English, Aligarh Muslim University

Humera Khatoon, Project Fellow,UGC Major Research Project, Department of English, Aligarh Muslim University

Sabina Kidwai, UGC Academic Staff College Course Participant, Jamia Millia Islamia, New Delhi

Introduction

This Volume of articles may be regarded, at one level, as a contribution to the field of Marginality Studies. For, central to almost all the articles in the Volume is the representation of Muslim woman in post-Independence Indian Writings in English (1950-2000). The Volume incorporates fruits of the study undertaken as part of the UGC Major Research Project awarded to me on the above topic. Needless to add, Muslim woman stands out as a typical marginalized entity in view of both her gender and for being part of the Muslim minority community in India. At another level, nonetheless, the present Volume seeks to amplify the points raised by Mushirul Hasan and M. Asaduddin in the "Introduction" to their selection of stories on Muslim lives in India.[1] In their prefatory note the editors express their hope that their anthology will help readers appreciate how these stories

> invoke and construct images of Muslims, offer a chronicle of our times, articulate many intimate yet historically unfamiliar points of reference, and represent the lived experiences of Muslims of different regions and socio-economic locations.[2]

Taking the cue from the above, the present Volume attempts to bring out the main contours of the representation of the Muslim woman in several Indian writings in English, including the stories included in the above-mentioned selection.

Another objective of this study is to examine whether this representation replicates or modifies, to any degree, the image of Muslim woman as ingrained in Western literary Orientalism. In so far as the representation of the Other, Norman Daniel makes this insightful observation:

> By misapprehension and misrepresentation an idea of the beliefs and practices of one society can pass into the accepted myth of another society in a form

> so distorted that its relation to the original facts is sometimes barely discernible. Doctrines that are the expressions of the spiritual life of an enemy are interpreted ungenerously and with prejudice, and even facts are modified – and in good faith – to suit interpretation.[3]

This fairly common human propensity to discredit the Other with a view to affirming one's own uniqueness, rather superiority, and to be swayed by misconceptions and stereotypes is reflected sharply in the representation of the Orient/Orientals in English literary texts, be these of the earliest or of our own times. The writings on the Orient are shot through with religious and cultural bias. The representation of one culture by another, as already stated, is liable to err; in the case of Western literary Orientalism the distortion is rooted in the unfortunate clashes – both ideological and military between the two major world faiths, Christianity and Islam.

The Songs of Geste and *The Song of Roland* provide the earliest instances of the presence of Oriental characters, women included, in Western literary tradition. Since *The Songs* are permeated with the crusading and missionary spirit of Christianity, these understandably conjure up a distorted image of Muslims. The misrepresentation born of deep hostility towards an Islam dismissed outright as a mere Christian heresy, consists not only in a disfiguring of Islamic creed but also in projecting a repulsive picture of Muslims. Perceived as the disciples of the devil, Muslims appear in *The Songs* as physical monstrosities, and as irrational people given wholly to violence and lust. Being non-Christian, rather un-Christian, they are seen as immoral, degenerate people indulging in cannibalism, polygamy and trading in women and slaves. As to the image of the Muslim woman in *The Songs*, as is pointed out by C. Meredith Jones, she is

> drawn largely from the imagination ... She seems to have no other object in life than to fall in love at first sight ... with a Christian knight whom she will eventually marry, and for whom she is eager to

> relinquish her religion. These ravishing and highly sensual ladies are not secluded or sheltered, but pitch their tents in the forefront of the armies so as to display their charms to the Christian heroes whom they are unable to resist. They are ready to sleep with them at once; they ceaselessly engineer opportunities for intercourse.[4]

In, at least, twenty *Songs of Geste* an Oriental/Muslim female readily converts to Christianity. She is usually the wife or daughter of an Oriental ruler who seduces a Christian knight, who, in turn, gallantly rescues her from the shackles of patriarchal tyranny. Philip Massinger's *Renegado* (1624) appears to re-echo the *Songs* in contrasting Christian purity with Muslim sensuality, and more importantly, in depicting Donusa, a Muslim princess who falls in love at first sight with Vitelli, a Christian dealer, and who recants her Islamic faith and offers her body to him in that "her religion allows all pleasure." Charmingly seductive harem women, ever-willing to abandon their faith and home, and elope with Christian lovers appear in Elizabethan and Restoration literature. Take Dryden's *Don Sebastian* (1691) as illustrative. Morayma, the Muslim jurisprudent's daughter, goes off with Antonio and utters derogatory remarks about her father's creed. Some remnants of the stereotype – an Oriental/Muslim woman reeling under tyranny, her segregation from men, her subjugation and being deprived of personal and sexual freedom – surface in Lord Byron's portrayal of Leila in his "Turkish Tale", *Giaour* (1813). Her attempt to break bondage brings only death upon her. Furthermore, she stands condemned and stigmatized for her departure from tradition. Not only Leila, Byron's other Oriental heroines too, namely, Gulnare in *The Corsair* (1814) and Gulbeyaz in *Don Juan* (1816) are no more than playthings or sexual objects in the sight of their husbands. Zuleika in Byron's *Bride of Abydos* (1813), brought up in patriarchal society displays total subservience to the male code of conduct. She is asked curtly by her father to get married to a total stranger, to which she readily consents. In sum, in Western literary Orientalism, Muslim woman is seen at the beck and call of masculine power. Her life is marred by the denial of freedom and her subjugation in every sense of the term, especially in sexual, social and political domains.

The present Volume seeks to identify whether Indian writings in English (1950-2000) retain, reinforce or break these stereotypes about Muslim woman.

The opening piece "Muslim Image in post-Colonial South Indian Fiction" by Masoodul Hasan, examines a broad range of literary works in English translation, originally written in Indian regional languages such as Malyalam, Kannada, Tamil, Telegu and Marathi, apart from writings of Manohar Mal gonkar, Anita Desai, Shashi Deshpande, and Shashi Tharoor in English. In Malyalam writings a note of cordial inter-community relations and syncretic tradition is observable. Some Kannada writers are found pointing to the tacit Dalit-Muslim understanding. Tamil stories tenderly relate the plight of the poorer sections of Muslims, with occasional streaks of anti-Muslim feelings. Telegu stories, however, offer a more positive and healthy image of Muslims. The note of Hindu-Muslim unity is to the fore in Marathi stories as well. In the English writings under study some Muslim characters display excellence in their respective fields, and hence command respect. They are perceived as beneficial for the larger society.

A.R. Kidwai's "(Un)veiling (Dis)honour: Image of Muslim Woman in Indian Writings in English" analyses a range of stories, originally written in post-Independence Indian regional languages, of which the English translations appear in the anthology *Image and Representation*[5]. Some of the stories retain faithfully the stereotype – Muslim woman subjected to onslaughts from both within and without. She is perceived as a captive, gasping for life within the stifling confines of her bigoted culture and religion, awaiting liberation and redemption. The Muslim religious practice of veiling is equated with death, which reduces young Muslim women into "living corpses". Her oppression at the hands of her ruthless, and callous husband lies at the core of several stories. Some other important issues raised in these writings are – the ignoble social practices and customs, which do not have any sanction in Islam, which have aggravated the plight of Muslim woman. These stimulating questions are brought into sharper relief mostly by Muslim story writers.

A.R. Kidwai's other piece, 'Imagining another Pakistan – Muqaddastan: Perception of Muslims in Balwant Gargi's *Purple Moonlight*' illustrates how a minority community is liable to be misperceived and distrusted. Gargi's some disturbing statements about the Muslim presence in India underscore the anxiety and precarious situation of the Muslim community.

Md. Mahmudul Hasan's "The Trope of Home and Representation of Muslim Women in Rokeya Sakhawat Hossain and in Attia Hosain's *Sunlight on a Broken Column*" tackles the issue of multiple meanings of home and of multiple modes of homelessness with its symbolic representation in the works of the two Muslim novelists under discussion. The paper relates woman's homeless condition to her gender and to the social norms of *izzat* (honour), which restrict her independence and impede her fulfilment as an individual.

Seemin Hasan's "Feminism and Feminist Utopia in Rokeya Sakhawat Hossain's *Sultana's Dream*," examining this early work (1905), draws attention to Hossain's critique on social inequalities faced by Muslim woman. Her works provide a pre-history to the later developments of feminism. More significantly, her utopian feminist fiction presents visions of a society without gender structures and inequal gender relationship.

Mohd Asim Siddiqui's "Suffering of Women and the Question of Plural Identity: Amitava Kumar's Reading of Politics of Faith in *Husband of a Fanatic*" studies Kumar's attempt to empathize with the ordinary suffering Muslim men and women. The focus is on the trauma experienced by them during communal riots. Kumar explores also the broader issue of religious identity, especially in the Indian subcontinent. His ideal of a plural identity is in a stark contrast with V.S. Naipaul's of "purity and fixity in religion". The paper yields illuminating points as Kumar probes the phenomenon of inter-community marriages.

Sami Rafiq's "Representation of Muslim Women in Qurratulain Hyder's *Agle Janam Mohe Bitia Na Kijo* and Ruskin Bond's *A Flight of Pigeons*: A Comparative Study" is essentially a comparative analysis of the two works set in different eras of Indian history, with their focus on Muslim woman. Both the texts underscore the suppression of women in the male dominated society. At the same time, these texts, especially of Hyder, adumbrate a female vision of reality and the hidden strengths of woman.

Humera Khatoon's "A Muslim Woman's Life in Qurrtulain Hyder's Fiction with Special Reference to *Sita Betrayed*, *The Housing Society* and *A Woman's Life*" explores further Hyder's perception of gender discrimination, of which Sita Mirchandani, Surayya, Manzurun Nisa, Rashke Qamar, and Jamilan are victims, notwithstanding marked differences in their socio-economic rankings.

Humera Khatoon's other piece "Muslim Women Characters in the Short Stories on Partition" focusses on Partition Literature in Urdu, Hindi and English, illustrating how women, in particular, bore the brunt of the tragedy flowing from the partition of India.

Notwithstanding being a critique on the representation in media/ television, Sabina Kidwai's "Image of Muslim Women in Indian Television Serials" in a sense, complements and supplements the main concern of the Volume – representation of Muslim woman. As in literary texts, in TV serials too, Muslim woman appears trapped miserably in the morass of overweening religious and socio-cultural restrictions.

An extensive Bibliography, compiled by Md. Mahmudul Hasan, encapsulates the discourse on the Representation/Gender issues, with pointed reference to Muslim woman.

Aligarh
August 2006

A.R.Kidwai
sulaim_05@yahoo.co.in

Notes and References

1. *Image and Representation: Stories of Muslim Lives in India*. Edited by Mushirul Hasan and M. Asaduddin, Delhi, Oxford University Press, 2000, p.6.

2. Ibid.

3. Norman Daniel, *Islam and the West: The Making of An Image*. Edinburgh, 1991, p.22.

4. C. Meredith Jones, "The Conventional Saracens of *The Songs of Geste*", *Speculum*, 17 (1942), p. 219.

5. *Image and Representation. Op. Cit.*

Chapter - 1

Muslim Image in post-Colonial South Indian Fiction

Masoodul Hasan

Literature is both a determiner and denominator of culture. As such it concerns itself with the individuals and inter-group equations and cross-responses of the people. With its infinite cultural resource the Indian pluralistic society offers a fertile area of literary study and evaluation of these mutual perceptions. Muslims with their unignorable demographic presence and momentous history in the subcontinent form the core of this majority-minority paradigm, frequently skewed by the insidious legacy of communal divide at the time of our independence. These circumstances have affected the Indian imagination and psyche. South Indian literary sensibility, expressed both in English and regional languages, has also registered these nuances.

Malyalam Novels

Historically, Muslims first recorded their presence on the Indian soil as Arab traders on the Malabar coast, and they have retained this mercantile character in Kerala. A famous modern Malyalam novel features a Muslim trader as its central character. Pareekutti, a successful Muslim trader, whose unrewarding love for Karuthamma, a struggling fisherman's pretty daughter, leads to his mental breakdown, and their death by drowning in a sea storm. *Chemmen* (1956) by Thakazaki S. Pillai won the President's Award and was translated into English by Narayana Menon under the same title in 1964.[1] Pareekutti arrived at her village, Nirkumman as a boy in the company of his father to make bulk purchases of shrimps. He wore trousers, a yellow shirt, "and a tasseled cap on his head" (p.6)—

the fez being the typical Muslim head gear. The impetuous Karuthamma struck an innocent friendship with him, and used to call him affectionately 'Kochumuthalali', a common friendly sobriquet for the Muslims. Her loving but wary mother cautioned her against the friendship as she was rather skeptical about the Muslims' sexual probity: " Some Kochumuthalalis with neither character nor decency defile the sea front. Low caste women come from inland to help at the curing yard, and sift the fish". (p.9) The unsavory imputation was obviously a common misunderstanding. Her own pride in caste and feminine uprightness is summed up in her advice to her daughter: " The strength and wealth of the fisherman lies in the purity of his wife."(p.9) Pareekutti advances a loan to Chamban, the girl's father, to help him purchase his gear and boat. This was, however, not done with any ulterior motives, as clarified by the narrator: "No, it could not be that. Parrekittu never tried to win Karuthamma by unfair means. He never wanted it that way" (Ch, 19; p.198); in fact, the young man's conduct confirmed the comment.

In keeping with tradition the unwilling Karuthamma is married to Palani, a hard working fisherman of a jealous and possessive nature, who does not allow his wife to visit her parental home even at the time of her mother's death. The love-lorn Pareekutti is deranged, and roams about the coast, singing songs of love. When he visits Chakki on her deathbed, she calls him her son, and asks him to look after Karuthamma as his sister. Later, Palani is caught in a sea-storm, as he goes shark hunting in the night. A fierce struggle with the predator-fish ensues which reminds the reader of Hemingway's Old Man's struggle with Marlyne. Palani perishes in the storm and in the meanwhile Pareekutti visits Karuthamma's house to help her, who is gone in search of her missing husband. Trying to rescue her from the sea-waves, Pareekutti is also drowned, and two days later their interlocked bodies are washed ashore. Their tragic end calls to mind the sad end of Heer and Ranjha and of Hero and Leander. Significantly, the final image of Pareekutti is that of a sincere, morally upright, tragic lover in conspicuous contrast to Chakki's impression about the erotic mis-demeanours of the Kochumuthalalis in general. Of course, the inter-community hiatus is very much there; the label of 'Otherness' still sticks to the Muslims, and inter community marriages with them are still frowned upon. But, otherwise they do not suffer from as blatant discrimination and disinformation as in other more populous parts of the country. Characteristically, the small-scale trade and commerce is still their favourite profession. Ahmad Kutty runs a tea-shop, and Hassan Kutty manages a provision-store. Khaddar is a middle-class fish-merchant, though commercial ethics is not his strong point. He resorts to undercutting and chicanery.

K.P. Ramamunni's *Sufi Pranja Katha* (1999) translated into English as *What the Sufi Said* (2002) by N. Gopalakrishan and R.E. Asher[2] is a densely constructed account of the emergence of a *Jarum* – a saint's tomb from the sea. It portrays the syncretical tradition of Keralite Muslims, and of the Sufi tolerance and liberalism as opposed to orthodoxy. Employing the technique of first-person narration, criss-crossed by the flash-back and dream devices, the non-Muslim protagonist here relates what he has learnt from the keeper of tomb at Mellepullarath which he had visited to make an offering. The story, located in the 19th century in the wake of a communal riot, has a contemporary relevance as well. The Sufic syncretism is articulated early in the novel in the tomb-keeper's opening remarks to the narrator: "The Beevis [Muslim women-saints] are all yours, my son, though you are a Hindu. And so also are all the Bhagwathys mine, though I am a devout Muslim. The first Beevi came from your community" (Ch.I, p.6) Karthy, the beautiful niece of a learned Brahmin landlord, Sanku Menon, lives with him along with her widowed mother. She is divinely blessed, and so immune to pestilence. When small pox breaks out as an epidemic, she attends the victims, unmindful of her own health or their low status and caste. Pithan Mamoothy, a Mapla from Ponnani arrives there on a business-trip, buys in bulk the coconut crop of Sanku Menon, and is allowed to stay in the latter's outhouse. Mamoothly is introduced in the novel as a "neo-rich Musalman.........[with] the short hair, the sprightly round beard, and the boat-shaped lips that kept up a steady smile even while standing there with the gravity and humility [a man of] quiet efficiency." (p.68) Karthy feels attracted towards him. Initially, he is indifferent, but gradually he also becomes interested in her. They elope to Ponnani,

Mamoothy swimming across the turbulent river with Karthy on his back. She is warmly welcomed at Ponnani, she embraces Islam, is named Sithara, and is married to her lover according to Islamic rites. Mamoothy is popular, highly respected in his home-town, and is a source of great help to his friends in their business transactions with the European merchants.

Karthy is loved by her in-laws, and is particularly close to Ayesha, Mamoothy's sister. She observes all the rites of Islam. At home, once she accidentally discovers an idol of a *devi*, buried in the ground, which she places is a niche in her chamber. Mamooty does not object to it, and is reported to have built a temple for it in his sprawling house. The local Imam, Avarumusaliar, however, protests and tries to create trouble. But Mamoothy firmly and successfully defies him. In the meanwhile some strange things happen, and mysterious fires break out in the house. The Imam, who himself is only a third-generation convert has some disturbing dreams, as his subconscious pagan memories revive, and he suffers from the tension of dual beliefs, and falls a prey to sleep-walking. Other superstitious people blame it on Mamoothy's apostasy, and his business associates terminate their deals with him. His poise and self confidence crack, a succession of failures follows, and he even grows indifferent to Karthy.

Syedumollakka, a religious leader, arrives on the scene, but failing in his self-appointed task of correcting Mamoothy, he conspires to kill the *Kafir* (lapsed Mamoothy). Beeran, Mamoothy's younger brother sends him out to sea on some business pretext, where he is murdered by the fanatical cohorts of Syedumollakka. In the meanwhile Karthy too, suffers nervous breakdown, and behaves abnormally. She cuddles Amir, her husband's nephew, performs some voodooistic rites with him, and walks into the Arabian sea. It was believed that her ghost sank the boat of her husband's murderers. A few days later, a severe storm broke out near Ponnani, and a fishing-boat capsized, but it was miraculously saved by a 'female form', supposed to be Kathy's spirit. The grateful fisherman buried the woman in sand; but as they turned homewards, they were mysteriously called back, and saw the mound of grave grow higher; a new *Jarum* was born. The village Imam confirmed its genuineness, as he had now come to believe in the miraculous advent of the saints. He organized the management of the new shrine, and from being a literalist he now turned into an illuminate - a Sufi. The author implies the harmonious confluence of *Shariat* and *Tariqat* here, which seems to be the call of times.

Towards the end the narrator asks the white-bearded keeper of the grave why the Beevis come again and again. He gives the following answer: "Son, shall I tell you why? Man is yet to acquire the ability to be good; But he always has desire to be good. It is this desire that appears from time to time as Beevis and Bhagwathys. When we forget one Beevi, a new Beevi appears." (p.170) This reply echoes the Muslim theory of the advent of the *Mujaddid* or the millennial reformer. The novel closes on an optimistic note that is particularly relevant in the present strife-riven and communally surcharged Indian scene today. The focus on the female saint in the novel may be a concession to the matriarchal culture of Kerala. The use of poetic imagery, symbolism and the tug of subconscious memory add to the literary quality of the work. Mamoothy's sagacious advice to Avarumusaliar before his own nervous breakdown sums up the author's view of Muslims and their faith: "No cultural or religious considerations could cast shadows where the light of the love and compassion of Allah shines." (p.117) Love and compassion is the cardinal feature of the Sufi message and ethics.

Malyalam Short Stories

The doyen of Malayalam fiction, Vaikom Muhammad Basheer's (1909-1994) 'Magic Strings'[3] deftly debunks the superstitions belief in magic - charms, and exposes the character of a phoney charm-seller, Zainul Abideen Thangal. Aziz purchases one to cure his own baldness and his dog's peculiar trait to bite Hindoo women only. The canine mischief may symbolically allude to a common misgiving about some Muslim youth's alleged philandering potential with communal overtones, while the much-vaunted charm-string fails Aziz on both these counts, his boyhood friend, Shanker Iyer, wins a handsome lottery by its virtue, his wife's labour-pains are eased, consequently he orders a fresh and plentiful supply of these charms. Apart from its satiric intention, the story brings out the mutual Hindu-Muslim cordiality at the individual level. Yet another Malyalam short story 'Mumbai' (1996)[4] by N.S. Mahadevan, a Sahitya Academy Award winner, sensitively hints at the vexatious discrimination against the Muslims in government offices, especially in the post-Bombay explosions (1993). Aziz, a Bombay-based Keralite, applies for a passport in order to go to the UAE. He is harassed and made to shunt from office to office on trivial pleas. He is directed to the Supply office to obtain a certificate of domicile, where an underling officer, Premila Gokhale, asks him for a certificate to the effect that he was in India in 1970, even though he had stated in his application that he was born in 1971. On this ground he is not only denied the passport, but the police hounds him on suspicion of being an illegal immigrant from Bangladesh. The story exposes not only the corruption and incompetence rampant in government offices, but it also suggests poignantly the bias and suspicion attached generally to the Muslim image. The anti-non-Maharashtrian feelings unleashed by the Shiv Sena in the state may also be noticed on the sidelines. A similar anti-immigrant bias is artistically exposed in another Malyalam short story 'Kabadi' (1991)[5] by a Delhi-based writer, Anand (P. Sachidanad; b 1936). Noor Mohammad, a junk-seller, lives in a jhuggi colony near Basti Nizamuddin, Delhi. The even tenor of these slum dwellers' miserable life is cruelly shattered by a communal riot over the issue of the forcible location of a crematorium on a plot abutting a Muslim cemetery. Noor Mohammad was twice displaced—once from Bihar, and later from East Pakistan. In the process he had lost two fingers, and one of his legs had to be amputated. In the latest Delhi riot he was shot dead by the police during curfew hours. The Bangladeshi syndrome has now become an identity tag of the floating Muslim population of the unemployed and the homeless. Anand takes a humanistic view, implying that the problem needs imaginative and compassionate handling.

Kannada Novel

Shiva Rama Kant's Kannada biographical novel (1959) translated into Urdu as *Maut ke Ba'd* (1974)[6] *After the Death* is a study in character.

Sick of property disputes in his family Yashwant Rao Hegde, an amateur painter, abandons his family and absconds to Bombay. He remarries there, and raises a small fortune. He has a paralytic stroke, but before his death he informs one of his friends—the narrator—at home of his will, and instructs that his modest legacy may be disposed of by him in a particular fashion. The friend diligently traces the address and performs his will. He meets a former neighbour of Hedge in Bombay. Ahmad ran a small shop in Bombay and was an admirer of Hegde. Dada, a personal servant of Hegde, was a cheat and fleeced him. Once he picked up a quarrel with Ahmad who in a fit of fury hit him on the head. Hegde chastised him, and admitting his lapse, Ahmad took Dada to the hospital and apologized. He also served Hegde in his illness and in his cremation. The author was much impressed by him, and wondered how he had kept true to humanistic values in the soul-searing, morally sordid atmosphere of Bombay, while Hegde's own children behaved most selfishly with him. The author appreciates and takes a positive view of Ahmad, as a non-descript representative of his community.

Another famous Kannada novel *Samaskara* by R. Ananthamurthy — translated into English by A.K. Ramanujan (1976)[7] and made into a commercial film in 1970 — also presents favourably a minor Muslim character. Narnappa, a well-to-do Brahmin of Durvaspura led a loose life. He lived out of wedlock with a low-caste woman, Chandri, and worse still, dined and drank with Muslims. His fellow Brahmins wished to excommunicate him, but stayed from doing so because of his threat to convert to Islam. He died of plague, and the caste Hindus refused to cremate him, even though they were put to a lot of inconvenience and hardship by the custom of abstaining from food as long as the corpse remained undisposed of. The body began to decay and stink. At last, a poor Muslim cartman, Ahmad Bari, helped Chandri to transport and cremate Narnappa's dead body secretly at a distant place from the village. Chandri also secretly saved another learned Brahmin from starvation on the same occasion, who in the privacy of night had no scruples about fondling a low caste woman's body. Other details of the plot portray the real *Samaskar* (spiritual transformation) of the learned Brahmin,

Pranesacharya. The novel is an allegory and protest against casteism, hypocrisy and hollow ritualism. Bari's helpfulness and human sympathy transcending considerations of caste or religion, derived from his faith, are noteworthy, as is the hinted potential of Dalit-Muslim cooperation, symbolised by Chandri-Bari collaboration at a critical time in the village.

The middle class Muslim culture and psyche are presented in a political Kannada novel of indifferent literary merit *Firdaus* (2003)[8] co-authored and translated by K.M. Aneesul Haq and Shylaja. It unfolds the evolution of a mildly modernized daughter of Ahmad Ali, a Commissioner at Bangalore. In a way the novel may be described as an exercise in defining modern Muslim self-image and identity, and contemplating a rather muddled and amateurish plan for the purpose. Thinly veiled references to persons and parties intersperse the novel, which is avowedly anti-ulema, anti-politician, anti-beaurucrat and anti-Aligarh in its views. Sir Syed Ahmad Khan is acknowledged as "a scholar and great writer", but his educational programmes his real *magnum opus* – is denounced vehemently. He is accused of establishing an institution only to produce "mental slaves", and to cater to the needs of the feudal class, though the scheme was opposed by the Muslim community as a whole. Further, according to the narrator, the AMU students not only migrated to Pakistan themselves, but they also encouraged other educated persons to migrate (p.46). In a parochial vein he states that while the alumni of AMU in Mysore and other states supported the demand for Partition, the alumni of the universities of Mysore and Madras stood for a united India (p.91) Ironically, the protagonist himself was all set for the migration but his wife Mubeena killed his resolve (p.42) Jigaryar Baig, an old boy of AMU was so intoxicated with liberalism that he "forced his females to mingle and adopt the Western style of life" (p.46). Ahmad Ali contested unsuccessfully election to the state legislative Assembly, and founded the Musawat Committee to secure political justice for Muslims. The novel gives an impression of being an essay in self-exculpation from the vicarious sin of Partition, and purports to explore some Muslim space in contemporary idea.

Firdaus is soft on Sufism, and contains a brief history of the Qadriah order (pp.54-62). The clairvoyant dervish in the *dargah* represents the universalist and human features of Sufism. The divorced and psychologically tense Firdaus is able to recover her serenity through the prayers of a Sufi at the tomb of Hazrat Baba Qadri. She is emotionally regenerated, and marries a second time. The Sufi is supposed to represent the human and pacific face of Islam, as distinguished from orthodoxy. The dervish even advises Firoz to "beware of Maulanas", not quite characteristic of the true Sufi.

Tamil Short Stories

A Tamil short story 'Tearless Eyes'[9] by Jamila shows the poverty and passion of a grave-digger. Kassim lived in the graveyard itself and was strong and handsome in his youth. Many years ago he used to supply water to his young cousin, Khatija, whom he married later. He loved Khatija passionately. She is struck by a mortal disease, and the impoverished husband does all he could for her treatment. The local *hakim* declares it a hopeless case, and Khatija asks him to dig her grave while she is alive; for she knows that after her death he would be too overwhelmed to be able to do so. He complies, and is struck with sorrow too deep for tears. Kassim represents the generally low economic status of the Muslims in Tamilnadu, and the practice of endogamous cousin marriages among them. The story looks like a projection of self-image and self-pity, as its author is a Muslim. Kassim's poverty would not permit him to look beyond the local *hakim* for better treatment of his wife. Another glimpse of Muslims' chronic economic deprivation in the South is given in "Father and Son" (1994) by Ashokamitran (p.193)[10] the narrator visits Secundarabad after thirty years, and tries to seek out his boyhood friend and playmate, Wahab, the son of a poor flower-seller at the railway station. The narrator was the son of a railway employee, and probably an Anglo-Indian. His other friend, Terence, from his own community looked down upon Wahab, and objected to his association with the narrator. He would often snub Wahab who read in an Urdu medium Islamia School. After much difficulty the narrator managed to locate a bearded flower-seller resembling Wahab's father of yester years. This old man was in fact Wahab himself, ravaged by time and poverty beyond recognition. Wahab's memory had also declined, and he fails to recognize his old playmate. He is the image of the poorer son of a poor father, symbolizing the general decline of the Muslims in the modern age. His Urdu-medium inadequate education and lack of initiative proved to be unshakable clogs; he is the prototype of a failed generation in the new dispensation. The portraiture is sensitive and sympathetic.

Thappil Mohamed Meeran (b.1944) wrote a Tamil short story 'The Vettamanglam Elephant' (1994)[11] which may be taken as an insider's first person account of the Muslim situation and psyche in southern Tamilnadu. The protagonist worked as an accounts clerk in a rice mill, where he accidentally discovered the financial irregularities of his supervisor, Naina, and is therefore subjected to harassment. In the meanwhile he requires to go home on leave to repair urgently his dilapidated house before the onset of monsoon. After much difficulty he obtains leave, but in the meanwhile he hears from his son, telling him of the likelihood of communal riots over the temple elephant's route to the sea for its annual ritual dip. The narrator boards the Jayanti Janta Express for his hometown, and has ominous visions of arson in his village. He contemplates a preventive, placatory move: "If I buy a garland as soon as I get off, and garland the elephant as it enters the town, the fire will, perhaps, be doused ... Or will it?" (p.145) The brief soliloquy sums up the minority's fears, exploitation, nagging poverty and sense of insecurity in its own land, and fairly represents the psyche of Muslims living in the shadow of abrupt communal eruptions.

Telegu Short Stories

Two Telegu stories deserve special notice for presenting a positive and genuinely sympathetic Muslim image. Sripada Subramanya Sastry's (1891-1961) 'Rose Attar'[12] associates refinement, self-respect and aesthetic sense with the Muslim central character in the story. Shukur Ali Khan is a perfumer from the north. He arrives at Peddapuram kingdom to present his excellent extract of rose-attar to the Maharaja. He meets the usual vexatious and bribe-ridden red tape, and has to bribe the functionaries and the Dewan of the state to fix up an interview with Maharaja. After several unsuccessful bids he is advised to wait for the ruler when he rides in a cavalcade. But, even this attempt fails. Feeling humiliated and frustrated, he flung the attar-bottle against the castle-wall, and since then the place has continually smelt of rose. Romance and legend intermingle in the story, but it leaves a positive impression of the attar-maker. Yet another story 'Deliverance' (1980)[13] by a Telegu engineer-writer, Nelluri Kesavaswamy (1920-1984) also offers a positive view of an educated Muslim youth. Sultan, the son of an aristocratic family and a student of AMU visits his home at Hyderabad during his summer vacation. As a prelude to his prospective marriage, his mother sends a coy, moon-faced servant girl, Shirin, to his bed-room to rehearse him in the conjugal game. Shocked and disgusted, he sends her back, but the embassy is repeated several times. Shirin tells him of his mother's pressure. At last Sultan yields, but resolves to make her his wedded wife. However, the family feels outraged by the proposal, and he is advised to follow the precedent of his elder brother who had dallied with another servant girl, Jugnoo, who was aborted and sent off. The idea is abhorrent to Sultan, and he decides to reject the degenerate culture. He writes to his history professor at Aligarh for a job, and pretends to toe the family line. Being a topper, he is offered a lectureship at the University and under the pretext of enjoying a pleasure trip with Shirin in Bombay, he leaves for Aligarh. From there he informs his mother of his marriage with Shirin. Sultan symbolizes the modern enlightened Muslim youth in revolt against some old, unhealthy customs. He declasses himself, obtains a respectable employment, rejecting his feudal, decadent, and parasitic heritage. He represents a new generation of Muslims with a healthy, positive outlook on future. The AMU and its mission has obviously contributed to this healthy change. N. Kesavaswamy justly debunks a perverse aspect of the decadent culture, but he does not hesitate to project a new dimension of the Muslim image.

A very different picture of poverty, ignorance and superstition emerges in another Telegu story 'The Home for the Peeroos'[14] by Kethu Viswanathaa Reddy (b.1939). The hold of 'Pirs' on the masses and their role as instruments of vote-bank politics makes the story's theme. Mastan, the Chief of the Peeroos, looks after a shrine which needs extensive repairs.

He is given to cock-fights, and his son, Vali, is no different in outlook and passivity. Mastan's help is courted by a political leader who promises the shrine's renovation, and Mastan's free medical treatment when he loses two fingers and a leg in an accident. The Chief Peero obliges his political wooer, who goes back on his electoral promises, when his candidate loses at the hustings, and even makes Mastan pledge an acre of land to him in part payment of the medical expenses. The exploitation may apply to other communities also, but the Peeroos' exceeding ignorance, wasteful habits and poverty make them particularly vulnerable. The saint veneration is yet another feature of some sections of Muslim society. At a deeper level, the dilapidated house/shrine represents the general decline in Muslim society, and its denial of self improvement, relying on hollow political promises for their amelioration.

Marathi Story

'Barso Ram Dharakey Sey', a Marathi story by Moinuddin Jinabade, appeared in translation in Urdu in 1966.[15] It strikes a nostalgic note, and revives hopes of Hindu-Muslim friendship. The protagonist who had migrated to Pakistan some fifty years ago, revisits Mumbai, where he had been born and brought up. He remembers and seeks out his boyhood friend, Thandi, with whom he used to play and sometimes, quarrel too. 'In the name of Ram' was Thandi's habit of speech and the Muslim boy used to tease him by repeating the speech tag, which was resented by Thandi who objected to its use by a Muslim. The narrator used to silence him by retorting, "So what? Why can't I call Ram even though I am a Muslim?" They even recall an incident when Thandi had hit the other boy on the head, that made him bleed. Years later Thandi's son married a Muslim girl whom her parents-in-law held in affection. Thandi's wife was a devout Hindu, yet she used to observe punctually the anniversary of Imam Husain's martyrdom with fervour. She would prepare the offerings, and call some pious Muslim to consecrate them with prayers. But in the year of Mumbai riots and blasts the offerings had to go unconsecrated, as no Muslim was forthcoming to say the prayers. Thandi went from mosque to mosque in search of one. But every time he was put off by the notices displayed in the mosques, banning the entry of members of other sects. The wife died soon after of the shock that her customary offerings remained unsanctified. This was disappointing to Thandi too, who was a genuine admirer of the martyrs of Kerbala, even though he considered himself a pure Hindu. The two friends bewail the communal eruptions and sectarian violence. The story is a statement of inter-faith amity, and suggests that every Pakistani Muslim need not be a Hindu-hater, nor every Indian Hindu a Muslim-baiter. The pointed mention of Ram in the title is specially significant in the background of the Ayodhya Movement in the name of Rama. The title has a symbolically evocative value as it is derived from a children's jingle:

Barso ram dharakey se *Budhya mar gayee faqey se*

[O Rama: let it rain in sheets / for the old widow dies of hunger and drought]

The drought and famine of love sweeps across the Indian subcontinent. Oceans of friendship and understanding alone can refertilize the arid earth. A Hindu and a Muslim child sing this chorus in the story. A refreshing Muslim image as the co-seeker of peace and amity emerges here in contrast to his identification with violence and terrorism.

English Novels

Monahar Malgonkar's political novel *The Princes* (1963)[16] is the story of an Indian prince's autocratic rule, luxurious life and his state's merger with the Union of India. It is a first-person narration by Abhaya Raj, the heir-apparent and thirty-nine-day Maharaja of the Bheel state of Begwad. Horji, the senior Maharaja, has two Muslims on his staff. Hamidullah, the supervisor of stables and riding-coach of Abhaya is an efficient officer, and excels in equestrian and training skills. Abdullah Jan, a handsome Police Officer of the Central Provinces is inducted in Begwad as the Captain of the Palace. He is a confidant of the Maharaja and his senior wife who enters into a liaison with him. Later, when he is sent back to his parent cadre, differences develop between the Maharaja and the Maharani. She retires to her parental estate in Jhansi, and calls back Abdullah Jan as its manager. Subsequently, she marries him. In the meantime the Partition of India takes place, and they migrate to Pakistan. She embraces Islam of her own free will, and makes some revealing statements in her valedictory interview with her estranged son, Abhaya, before her migration to Pakistan. She tells him: "I am happy, happy because I have found that I have a place of honour in a man's house. I am the wife, the lady of the house, a sharer in the joys and sorrows of the husband. Here I was nothing." It may be an individual experience, but it also sounds like a testimony to the respect and rights of the wife in the Muslim family. About her conversion she adds: "And I can assure you that I did not become a Mahommedan because he wanted me to, but because I wanted to belong to my husband's religion, belong completely to him... hold nothing back that I had to give." (p. 335)

In her self-justification she also makes a statement that reflects the common misconceptions that Muslims are psychological aliens in India – and by implication that Pakistan is their emotional anchor, as India is supposed to be the land of Hindus only. Abhaya protested: "But you cannot go there, Maji. It is foreign territory now. They are killing thousands of Hindus everyday. It is here you belong. With us..." (p. 334). She rejoined: "No, I don't belong here. I belong there, on the other side of the border" (p. 334). These feelings were understandable in the immediate aftermath of the Partition. Passage of time has assuaged them considerably, though the pace of transition still leaves much to be desired.

Two minor female characters in the novel are also sketched on positive lines. Amina is the favourite keep-girl of the senior Maharaja. She is graceful, soft-spoken and well grounded in music. Even the difficult-to-please Abhaya Raj holds a good opinion about her. She is intelligent and "almost refined even though she never learned to read or write." (p. 57). True to her upbringing, she invites her niece, Zarina, to raise her as the future comforter of the prince. Both the girls show exquisite courtly manners. Even concubinage has not defiled their natural grace.

Malgonkar has utilized his personal military background to his advantage, and touched upon the theme of Indo-Pakistan tensions in a couple of his later novels also – the *Bandicoot Run* (1982) and *The Garland Keepers* (1987). Spying and intelligence is their forte, but his *Cactus Country* (1992) about the Bangladesh war presents some well-drawn Muslim characters. Aslam and Pirzada, officers in the Pakistan Army, are treated with particular attention. Aslam's mother was a Sikh by birth, but she was devoted to her Muslim husband. Possibly she is a later day version of the senior Maharani of Begwad of *The Princes*. She receives affection in her husband's household. Major Prizada was a Bengali by birth, and therefore, torn by conflicting loyalties to the Army and his motherland. But patriotism prevails over professional considerations. This is a particularly significant note in the background of some ill-conceived notions of Muslims' suspected imbalance between nationalistic and religious values.

Anita Desai

Anita Desai's *In Custody* (1984)[17] attempts a serious and, on the whole, sympathetic study of Urdu culture commonly associated with Muslims. Deven Sharma teaches Hindi in a mofussil college at Mirapore, but he has a passion for Urdu poetry. On the suggestion of his friend, Murad, an amateur journalist, he undertakes to write a biography of the renowned poet, Nur Shahjahan Abidi. Deven wants to tape an interview with Nur, which the whimsical and elusive poet almost thwarts on several occasions. Nur is a gourmand and a besotted bohemian – the traditional image of the Urdu poet – and is fond of Mughalai dishes. Deven tries to meet his demands to the best of his ability, and is even financially exploited by Nur's senior Begum. Murad is a parasite on his father, and his dubious journalistic projects come to naught. He represents the present day luxury-loving, mammon-struck youth, of whom there is no dearth in Muslim society either. Abid Siddiqui is lecturer in Urdu in Deven's College but he has little love for the language, and is enamoured of consumerist culture. Paradoxically, while Deven, the Hindi teacher, incurs debt and neglects his family to write on an Urdu poet, Abid sells his ancestral property and invests in real estate. Though no positive picture of Muslim character emerges in the novel, at least a general attitude of upward exertion on their part is reflected here. Unlike their fictional predecessors, none of Anita Desai's Muslim characters suffers from the Partition - syndrome. Also they show a healthy trend for financial advancement and independence. This is also borne out by the character of Habibullah in *Baumgartner's Bombay* (1988) who manages his timber business well despite riots and arson in Calcutta. In *In Custody*, however, Desai shows her concern for Urdu language and culture, particularly dear to the Muslims.

Anita Desai provides some realistic perspectives of the ill-conceived Urdu-Hindi animus, and the decline of Urdu, mainly because of the apathy and visionlessness of its self-styled guardians. The snobbish Murad makes a hollow lament: "who reads Urdu any more" (p. 15), and refers derisively to Hindi as "that vegetarian monster" and "the language of peasants" (p. 15). Abid Siddiqui indulges in sharp satire: "Yes, Urdu is becoming a rarity – it is only grown for export. To Pakistan, or to the Gulf. Have you heard Faiz has gone to Beirut, to edit an Urdu magazine?" (p. 97)

While some Urdu-wallas revel in their ineffectual anti-Hindi tirade and coo in self-pity, the anti-Urdu lobby does not spare their fangs either. Trivedi, Deven Sharma's Head of the department, takes the latter to task for his pro-Urdu stance: "I'll see to it you don't get your confirmation. I'll get you transferred to your beloved Urdu Department. I won't have Muslim toadies in my department, you'll ruin my boys with your Muslim ideas, your Urdu language. I'll complain to the Principal, I'll warn the RSS, you are a traitor." (p. 145)

Desai has aptly encapsulated the middle class Muslim image in popular imagination. He is given to tall talk, glories in his past, is averse to reality, and generally indulges in self-pity. There is even an ominous warning about the demise of Urdu culture, its replacement by a new ethos unless people awaken to the danger, and activise themselves in a constructive manner. A bitter question suggests itself – Is Urdu the notorious *femme fatale*, bringing its own custodians to grief? Be that as it may, Anita Desai has portrayed a realistic image suffused with enlightened sympathy.

Shashi Deshpande

Shashi Deshpande's *Small Remedies* (2000)[18] is mainly the story of two extraordinary women – a musician and a social activist. Madhu, an upcoming journalist, is commissioned to write the biography of Savitribai Indorekar, the singing legend of the times. Her biographer is to take sessions with the ailing enigmatic Bai to collect material for the work. While exploring the subject, Madhu interweaves into it the life-story of her maternal aunt, Leela, a devoted communist. In the process Madhu brings in shreds of her own life shattered by the death of her teen-aged son, Aditya, in a road-side bomb blast. Two minor Muslim characters criss-cross her own life. Hamid Merchant, the proprietor of the *City News*, and patron of an art group 'The Bombay Aficianadoes', gives her a start in life by appointing her the editor of his paper. He was a cultured, genial, public-spirited person, and in spite of his English suit, unmistakably a Muslim" (p. 104). He came of a nationalist family, and his own patriotism was never in doubt. His business acumen was sharp, his philanthropy patent, and yet he led a simple life (p. 160). When Madhu was desperately in need of accommodation for herself, he generously accommodated her in his own family house (p. 85). She, however, has unpleasant memories of another Bombayite, Marathi-speaking Muslim colleague, Dalvi. Deferential – even obsequious – to his boss, Dalvi shows traits of suppressed anti-feminism and was a source of gender-harassment to Madhu.

Two consanguinous Muslim characters play a crucial role in Savitribai's life. Like Shakespeare's Caesar, Ghulam Saab scarcely appears on the stage, and yet he largely dominates the course of Bai's life. He was a *tabla*-accompanist and instructor, who finally eloped with her to freedom and stardom. He helped Bai financially, and was sincerely devoted to her, even neglecting his own family. His daughter squarely blamed Bai for it: "That woman squeezed my father's heart like an orange" (p. 275). It was rumoured that he took to heavy drinking, but when he rejoined his family because of Bai's coldness, he gave up drinks. His granddaughter testified: "He had always been a devout Muslim, now his entire life seemed to be governed by the religious code" (p. 274). He was the best *tabla* player in his day, and the guru of the reigning artiste of the day, Shivaji. Again, in the words of his granddaughter, herself an accomplished singer, "He was incomparable, *la jawab* ... there was no one with his skill or knowledge ... His fingers were magical, they could weave complex *taal* with ease and fluency" (p. 273). In spite of all these accomplishments Ghulam Saab practised humility: "He did not play the game of one-upmanship as many *tabla* players do now" (p. 273). The description and praise is almost lyrical.

For some unexplained reason Ghulam Saab's daughter Munni by Savitribai hated him, and chose to call herself the daughter of Bai's husband, Joshi. Ghulam Saab loved Munni dearly, and was said to have taken to drinks only after Munni left for Pune. Equally, inexplicably Bai was too cold to Munni. Possibly, Munni did this to avenge her neglect by her mother.

Hasina was Ghulam Saab's daughter's daughter. She trained with Bai for 15 years, and lived with her for two years. She even taught the students on Bai's behalf. She attended lovingly on Bai in her last illness. Urdu was her mother tongue, yet she spoke perfect Marathi. In view of her accomplishments she was slated to sing in the temple of Bhivanipore in the main festival. Some other famous Muslim musicians had enjoyed the honour in the past. Her programme was announced, but suddenly objections were raised to a Muslim's participation in the concert. Anti-Muslim feelings were aroused by fanatics, which was inevitable in the background of communal riots. But, Ravi, the organizer of the programme stuck to his guns. Hasina was allowed the honour. She sang the bhajans rapturously till dawn. Madhu's tribute to her singing is heartfelt: "As Hasina sings the *Malkaus*, which she does in a meditative, reflective mood, I remember her at *Namaz*. She is giving the same intense concentration that she gives the physical motions of prayer, she brings the same total absorption to this *raga* that she brings to her prayers". (p. 138)

These are appreciative glimpses of an individual at peace and in harmony with her denominational as well as national settings, giving the lie to lurking suspicions about her coreligionists' national moorings.

Shashi Tharoor

Though brought up and educated outside Kerala, Shashi Tharoor's Malyali stock qualifies his English novel to be included in the South Indian fiction. His multi-motif recent novel, *Riot* (2001)[19] presents the current Indian communal psyche with objectivity and insight. The composite narrative strategies of media notices, investigative journalism, personal journal entries, letters and official interviews interweave episodes of passionate inter-racial love with acts of communal violence and murder of an American girl, Priscilla's murder in Zalilgarh, a town near Delhi, in 1988. He paints the Muslim situation and bruised psyche with sympathy in the background of the communal hype on the issue of Babri Masjid/Ram Janam Bhoomi controversy. Hindu fanatics' low and hostile view of the Muslims in general is projected through the vitriolic statements of Ram Charan to Randy Diggs, the American journalist. They are blamed for adhering to a faith of foreign origin, for outbreeding the Hindus, and for wangling dubious advantages from "Muslim-loving rulers like that brown Englishman Jawaharlal Nehru" (pp. 54-55). Ram Charan caustically concludes, "Muslims are like a lemon squirted into the cream of India." (p. 57)

A more factual perspective, however, is provided by the honest District officers – Lakshman, the District Magistrate and Gurinder Singh, the Superintendent of Police – in their interviews to Priscilla, the American working with an NGO on a project of population awareness in the town. Lakshman blames it all on debased politics, and finds it sheer insanity and rank injustice "to make Muslims pay a price for what Muslims may have done a hundred-fifty years ago" (p. 145). Gurinder deplores the rashness of "a bunch of Muslims" deciding to make sutli-bombs "to retaliate against all the insults and provocations flung their way by Hindu extremists" (p. 150). Tharoor does not gloss over the ignorance and bigotry of a few

Muslims misled by the belief that Islam is in danger. Ali, the short-tempered car-driver, is dead against family planning, and ill-treats his wife, Fatima bai, a mother of seven. Fatima, however, shows more common sense and moral courage – as against the general low impression about Muslim women's obscurantism and docility in the face of oppression – and she aborts her eighth pregnancy in consultation with Priscilla. Shashi Tharoor also delineates sympathetically the helplessness and grouse of Muslims at the discriminatory punitive action against them by the law-enforcing agencies in times of communal outbreaks, even though the former are invariably at the receiving end. (pp. 173 and 178).

In the novel Professor Sarwar, the historian is a picture of sanity and objectivity. He represents the sober aspect of the Indian Muslims' character. He briefly traces the historical view of Sri Ram controversy with balance and precision, and even hints at the contributory "role of Islam in the sanctification of Rama" (p. 182). The Professor, the two officers – particularly, Gurinder – and Priscilla, who falls in love with Lakshman, are treated deftly. She comes to a violent end during the curfew hours, and is found murdered at the place of her usual rendezvous with Lakshman. The unsolved mystery of her murder, pointing the needle of suspicion in three different directions, adds a fresh dimension to the novel. Sarwar's patriotism and clarity of thought are best summed up in his cool analysis of history and the heart-felt quotation from Iqbal, calling upon Indians to beware of the machinations of their foes (p. 258). Shashi Tharoor paints the fear and persecution complex and the occasional rash reactions of the Indian Muslims with understanding and sensitivity, but without endorsing the consequences of their panic reactions.

It may not be fair to attempt generalizations on the basis of a limited study. But some interesting points emerge even from this tentative study of a few works of South Indian fiction. Bhisham Sahni has commented on the thinning out of Muslim presence in the post-Independence Hindi short story.[20] The process, however, seems to have reversed in the case of South Indian fiction. Quasi-Muslim themes and characters appear to have gained in frequency. Writers from Kerala have highlighted the sense of amity and closeness among the fisher-folk of the region, where often inter-community marriages are tolerated, though nascent signs of fanaticism under revivalist influences from the North are also sometimes in evidence. The discrimination against Muslims by inefficient and corrupt officials in metropolitan towns is skillfully exposed, but the dominant syncretic tradition of Kerala survives undiminished. Concern for the underdog and the Muslim slum-dwellers in the North, haunted by the fear of being dubbed as illegal migrants and their actual victimization during riots is a reality. Some Kannada works hint at the tacit Muslim-Dalit cooperation and mutual help in crises, and show a strongly nationalist strain – with an occasional anti-Pakistan tirade – amidst the potential of sufism and syncretism. Tamil stories treat tenderly the life of indigent Muslims like the grave-digger or the balloon-seller, and the fear of endemic communal eruptions on petty issues. Faint rumblings of intolerance of the North during 1990s, though not of the same intensity, are audible in some stories. Telegu short stories offer a more positive and healthy image. The character of a self-respecting master-perfumer is difficult to forget, as is the social amelioration and progressive declassing achieved by a youth educated at Aligarh. At least one Marathi story makes out artistically a strong case for Indo-Pak amity, and reflects the basic unity of the two peoples. These are happy omens of a positive inter-community understanding and harmony. Surprisingly, all of them came from across the Vindhiyas.

A word may be added about the English novels treated here. Unlike the regional stories, these works portray the middle class. Their major Muslim characters are virtuosos – an eminent Urdu poet, a master-musician and a learned historian. This association of excellence, on however small a scale, with a minority, avowedly backward, symbolizes a genuine respect for them, and holds promise of a mutually beneficial regard for each other. But this trend of understanding and consideration must percolate down the line to the average man in order to be really meaningful in a wider sense.

Notes and References

1. Thakazadi S. Pillai, *Chemmen*, tr. By Narayana Menon, Jaico Publishing House, Bombay, 1964 (1968 reprint). All references to the novel are from this edition. Page numbers are given within parentheses in the text itself. The same style of reference is followed in the case of other works.
2. K.P. Ramamunni, *Sufi Pranja Katha* (tr. into English as *What the Sufi Said*), Rupa and Co. New Delhi, 2002.
3. V.M. Bashir, 'Magic Strings', (in Mushirul Hasan and M. Asaduddin (ed.) *Image and Representation*: *Stories of Muslim Lives in India*, Oxford University Press, 2000.
4. N.S. Mahadevan, 'Mumbai' (in *ibid*).
5. Anand, 'Kabadi' (in *ibid*).
6. Shiva Ramakant, *Maut ke Ba'd*, National Book Trust, New Delhi, 1974.
7. U.R. Ananthamurthy, *Samaskara*, tr. By A.K. Ramanujan, OUP, New Delhi, 1976.
8. M.A. Haq and Shylaja, *Firdaus – A Novel,* Hasman Pub. House, New Delhi, 2003.
9. Jamila, 'Tearless Eyes', *The Plough and the Stars*, ed. K. Swaminathan, Asia Pub. House, 1963.
10. Asokamitran, 'Father and Son' (in Mushirul Hasan, *op. cit.*)
11. Thappil M. Meeran, 'The Vethanmanglam Elephant' (in Mushirul Hasan, *op. cit.*)
12. Sripada S. Sastry, 'Rose Attar' in *A Generation of Telegu short Stories* (tr. By M.V. Sastry). International Telegu Inst., Hyderabad, 1965.

13. Neeluri Kesawswamy, 'Deliverance' (in Mushirul Hasan, *op. cit.*)

14. K.V. Reddy, 'The Home for the Peeroos' (in *Ibid*)

15. M. Jinabarde, 'Barso Ram Dharakey Sey' in *Saughat*, Urdu periodical, Bangalore, March, 1996.

16. Manohar Malgonkar, *The Princes – A Novel*, Hamish Hamilton, London, 1963.

17. Anita Desai, *In Custody,* Heinemann, London, 1984.

18. Shashi Deshpande, *Small Remedies,* Penguin Books, 2000.

19. Shashi Tharoor, *Riot: A Novel*, Penguin Books, 2001.

20. See 'Introduction' in Balraj Sahani (Compiled), *Anthology of Hindi Short Stories*, (Tr. By Jai Ratan), Sahitya Akademi, Delhi, 2003.

Chapter - 2

(Un)veiling (Dis)honour
Image of Muslim Woman in post-Independence Indian Writings in English

A.R. Kidwai

In their prefatory note to the anthology, *Image and Representation: Stories of Muslim Lives in India*, (New Delhi, Oxford University Press, 2000, p. 6) the editors express their hope that their selection of stories will help readers grasp how these stories

> invoke and construct images of Muslims, offer a chronicle of our times, articulate many intimate yet historically unfamiliar points of reference, and represent the lived experiences of Muslims in different regions and socio-economic locations.

This paper is an attempt to analyse some of the stories included in this anthology along the above lines, especially in terms of indicating the main contours of their representation of Muslim woman.

> Tripping on the torn seam of her ghaghra she ran quickly through narrow paths that turned into corners at every few steps. (p. 290)

The above opening sentence of Vishwapriya L.Iyengar's (b. 1958) story "The Library Girl"[1] encapsulates, in a sense, the image and representation of Muslim woman in contemporary Indian writings in English. In the above description she is perceived as an insecure, weak person exposed to onslaughts from both within and without. Worse, she is seen as a captive, gasping for breath within the suffocating confines of her bigoted culture and religion, and awaiting liberation and redemption. Vishwapriya L. Iyengar, a lady journalist and social activist, assumes this mantle in narrating the plight of Muslim woman. So doing, she spawns the errors common in the Orientalist perspective on Islam and Muslims. For her story, "The Library Girl" conjures up all the stereotypes and misperceptions about Muslim life – heartless, tyrannical father as the head of the patriarchal family and society, who is heavily biased against the female gender and believes in her inferior status as an article of his faith; voiceless, timid and suffering generations of Muslim women and the grotesque, rather morbid way of life in a Muslim *basti* (locality).

Central to "The Library Girl" is the pitiable story of a withering bud – Talat, a young, vivacious Muslim girl who is keen on pursuing education. She is rudely denied this basic right by her gender-biased, oppressive father who forces her into abandoning her education and imposes on her the donning of *burqa* (the long black outer garment worn by Muslim women for covering their body when they go out of home). Talat's mother and grandmother resent her initiation into this centuries-old custom. However, being victims of similar injustice perpetrated against them down the ages by the patriarchal Muslim society, they are too weak and helpless even to voice a note of their dissent or protest. As mute spectators they watch Talat's subjugation. After donning *burqa*, Talat realizes to her utter dismay and shock that she has been divested of her identity. She thinks she stands shorn of recognition and individuality. For, after donning *burqa* she is not recognized by the very men, both old and young, who lusted after her. The security and privacy accruing from *burqa* is dismissed by Iyengar as a serious blow to her identity and honour. The story challenges, rather rejects disdainfully the Islamic socio-religious practice of *Hijab* or *burqa* which aims at protecting female identity and honour by way of keeping her away from the lustful male gaze. The story thus represents the polarization of binary perspectives on female identity and honour.

At a very young age, Talat is barred from school education owing to her father's meagre resources. Not only is his father illiterate and incapable of raising his family, he is responsible also for keeping her daughter illiterate. He is behind the times on more than one count. What is most rankling is that he is grossly gender-biased. For, he somehow manages to raise money for his son, Tahir's education. However he has got "none for Talat's" (p. 292). When his wife disapproves such blatant discrimination, he audaciously tells her: "Buy her silk, satin, velvet, silver, but, foolish woman, don't compare her with Tahir" (p. 292). For him, girls are destined only for doing household chores, a role assiduously performed by his wife. Throughout the story his wife exists only on the margins, "slashing the meat" in the kitchen (p. 292), and rubbing "rock-salt on the goat's leg". In the process, "her long, thick fingers were a little blood stained" (p. 292). Later on, she injures her thumb in cutting "the meat that had not yet softened". (p. 294). She thus personifies, in a sense, the sacrificial goat at the altar of traditional Muslim way of life. She is bruised both physically and emotionally. Passivity and submissiveness are common to all the three generations of Muslim women in the story – the grandmother, mother and Talat. On seeing that the father had brought a *burqa* for the young Talat:

> Grandmother's old fingers knotted the white thread. Ammi [Talat's mother], rubbed rock-salt on the goat's leg. (p. 294)

The women's disapproval and disgust underscores further their inability to take any step. They are so repressed that it is beyond them to resist what they reckon as gross injustice. As the father, whose eyes shone with pride and pleasure on placing his young daughter within *burqa*, points to the beautiful glass crystals adorning the burqa,

> Her mother rubbed salt into the goat's breast and did not know if glass crystals were not being rubbed into her own eye. The old woman dropped her eyes onto a crotched flower. (p. 294)

When Talat puts on the new *burqa* for the first time, Iyengar's revulsion reaches new heights:

> She [Talat] turned to the mirror. A wooden eagle held the mirror between its claws. Ammi took out her long black iron knife and began to rub salt into the rust spots at the

> tip. She saw her beautiful sun and star child become night in the mirror.
>
> Talat saw her own veiled face in the mirror and felt afraid. She had also seen her mother's face. In the cage the crows had died. (p. 294)

The symbols – rubbing salt into the breast, glass crystals rubbed into the eye, the eagle with its claws, long black iron knife, rust spots, the beautiful sun and the star child becoming night and the crows dying in the cage – accentuate the misery plaguing the lives of Muslim women – their victimization, their suppression, their helplessness, the benighted darkness enveloping them, their captivity and their life-in-death.

Equally revolting and suffocating is the locale of Talat's existence – the Muslim *basti* (locality), with rats lying "dead on the circular iron lid of the sewer" (p. 291). More loathsome are the hide shops dotting the *basti*:

> Brown, dry hides in the exact shape of a goat. The neck and the four legs all sewn up. (p. 292)

These hide shops are reflective of the morbidity which permeates the characters and site of the story. The "sewn up" body of the goat is intended to heighten the grim reality of Talat's gagged life. She hates her house, consisting of "bare walls". In the library she "loved to see aeroplanes, truck, and women working in the fields." (p. 293). Her desire to escape, rather abandon her ancestral town, culture and faith is too strong. She looks forward to a saviour who might liberate her from her shackles. Not unsurprisingly, "Talat liked to read about the people who change things that seemed unchangeable" (p. 293). As a Muslim woman she is incapable of changing her own lot. Nor is there any hope of a redeemer ever emerging in the sterile, sordid Muslim *basti*.

She is destined for endless suffering. Wrapped in her *burqa* when she visits the library, she discovers to her fury that the *burqa* has divested her of her identity. For she is not recognized as Talat by the ogling young men on the street or the lecherous old Asad baba. Yet she loathes her *burqa*:

> Within the veil, a darkness seized Talat. It bandaged her mouth, her eyes, and sealed her voice.
>
> Talat cried and Talat screamed inside her black veil. But they did not hear and did not see. (pp. 295 and 296).

How ironic it is that she curses and rejects the device which accrues to her privacy, identity and security. The writer's convoluted thought in this instance is somewhat paradoxical.

The Telugu story writer, Khaja's (b. 1969) diatribe against veil in his story "Haram"[2] (1997) is even much more pronounced and virulent, as is evident in this passage reminding one of a rather sensationalistic, journalistic piece:

> The burqa not only covers the Muslim women's bodies, but also their dreams, their appearance, and their age, and what's more, it completely obliterates their very existence and brings in that much of darkness. Relationships mean nothing where burqas are covered. All acquaintances become non-acquaintances. It's difficult for anyone to make out who is beneath the burqa, difficult perhaps even for Allah. (p. 328)

The story is centred on Abdul, a promiscuous gang leader who spent all his time on

> ogling at the fresh flowerlike bodies of the Hyderabadi girls … or leaning against girls in a crowded bus and whether the driver braked suddenly or not falling all over them in the heat of youth… (p. 326)

One day he targets some young women in *burqa*. He is drawn, in particular, to one of them and deliberately bumps into her. However, he gets no response from this *burqa*-clad woman. On reaching home the first thing which that woman does is to hurl her *burqa* into fire. For it was her son Abdul who had tried to molest her, failing to recognize her in *burqa*.

The story denounces not only *burqa* but almost all that is associated with Islam and Muslims. The diminutive form "Abdul" as used of the main character, implies the author's reluctance to grant him the status of an ordinary, normal human being. The diminutive form aims at belittling and degarding him. The author's design to dehumanize Abdul is reflected also in comparing him and members of his gang to the menacing "wasps" (p. 326). Their perversion or lust for the female body borders on almost abnormal:

> They could survive for ages even on islands which did not have any food or water, but they could not stand even half a moment at a place without a young woman. (p. 327)

The story reiterates forcefully the stereotype of the lustful Muslim male. Abdul does not spare his own mother. Nor are his gang members averse to molesting their coreligionist Muslim women in *burqa*:

> Five or six sprightly young women got in. All in burqas!
>
> The spirits of Abdul and his gang revived.
>
> 'Hey', they are birds from "our" flock, Abdul said. 'That's good because we have been bored all this while in the bus', said another. (p. 328)

Sniffing and running after the female flesh is the only preoccupation of Abdul and his gang:

> While one wanted to go to the movie, another didn't – they went on arguing. In fact, they moved around without a definite programme. They kept changing their plans, depending upon whether they found young women or not. (p. 327)

Besides *burqa*, other Islamic sanctities too, are derided in "Haram". The sight of the overcrowded city buses brings to the author's mind the Hajj, Islamic pilgrimage, especially the chaos and mob frenzy during the Hajj as perceived by him: "The stampede which would take place once a year in Mecca was a routine occurrence in Hyderabad's city buses in the evenings." (p. 327) It is indeed a pity that Hajj, a salvific journey which accrues to pilgrims numerous benefits – spiritual, social, economic and intellectual, is equated only with unruly mob frenzy. This reminds one of a similar attack directed against Hajj in Jean P. Sasson's pulp novel representing hate literature, *Princess Sultana's Daughters* (New York, Bantam Books, 1994). Sasson exerts herself in divesting Hajj of its halo and spirituality in speaking of it, in a refrain-like manner, as a 'chaotic affair", "pandemonium" (p. 78) and "the dreaded effects of four million frenzied worshippers bent on trampling, crushing and killing fellow pilgrims in this dangerous religious ceremony." (pp. 81, 83 and 84).

The author associates *burqa*, both literally and metaphorically, with death, reducing a woman to "a living corpse". *Burqa* is referred to as shroud, an essential part of Muslim burial practice. While the latter covers the dead body, the former sniffs out a Muslim woman's dreams and life. Throughout the story "Haram", the leading female character does not speak a single word, though the entire action is centred around her. Inside her *burqa* she has only a shadowy presence. Even when Abdul pleads his innocence for bumping into her, as a pretext for gaining acquaintance with her,

> she did not speak. With utmost difficulty she lifted the eyelids she had closed centuries ago. There was sadness in those eyes. Disgust, tiredness, weakness, a sense of being subjugated, a latent sorrow, tears in the corners of her eyes. (p. 329)

Nonetheless, she is seen taking a bold, decisive step at the end of the story – of consigning her *burqa* into fire. It is hard to make out why her *burqa* bears the brunt for Abdul's depravity and debauchery. Had she or any other female not been clad in *burqa*, would she have escaped molestation at Abdul's hands in a society in which women routinely face dishonour and degradation at every step in their lives? The reason for singling out *burqa* and denouncing it appears to be rooted in the stereotype that *burqa* is Muslim women's bane. A veiled Muslim woman is envisioned as in numerous other texts of Western literary Orientalism, as a sacrificial lamb betrayed by its master:

> Something like surprise was seen in her eyes like that of a goat at the point of being cruelly slaughtered by the very master who tended it with care. (p. 329)

Similar stereotypes recur in Ashokamitran's (b. 1931) "Father and Son".[3] It nostalgically relates the protoganist's friendship during his school days with a Muslim class fellow, Wahab. Nonetheless, Wahab is introduced as "the chap with filthy clothes who kept spitting all over." His little house with "a small entrance was always covered with a screen of torn sackcloth" (p. 240). Equally disgusting is Wahab's sister:

> There were black patches under her eyes, … She was about twelve or thirteen but looked thin and emaciated, with shoulder bones sticking out. I wondered how on earth she was able to stand on her legs. (p. 241)

Wahab's other family members – his brother and mother – are repulsive in both moral and social terms:

> That day there was a big commotion in his house. His brother had quarrelled with his mother who, in a fit of temper, threw a ladle at him. She missed her target and the brother picked it up and flung it back at her, injuring her forehead. As blood quashed out of the wound, Wahab took his mother to the Municipal Hospital. (p. 241)

The binary opposition between "us" and "them" comes out sharply in projecting the latter as nothing short of beasts:

> We quarrelled at home but nobody thought of using a ladle as a weapon. Our fights stopped with verbal exchanges. (p. 241)

The agony suffered by Wahab's sister and mother as helpless victims of the injustice perpetrated against them in the male-dominated Muslim society is a recurring feature of the Indian writings in English on Muslim lives.

In Mohan Parmar's (b. 1948) "Metamorphosis"[4] (Gujarati, 1996) one meets Shakilabanu, wife of Rahim Khan as another victim of similar domestic violence. Rahim Khan appears as a typical Muslim male – an irrational brute, deviod of tender feelings and emotions and given only to violence and bloodshed:

> Rahim Khan ran around the house like a mad man, picking up whatever he could lay his hands on and dashing them violently at the wall and on the floor. Shakilabanu screamed. He pounced on his wife and started beating her up with a can. The house turned into a battle field. She ran to avoid further blows. But Rahim Khan came right behind her and hit her at will. (p.176)

More significantly, this damsel in distress gets comfort and consolation at a Hindu temple, Hunaman Mandir:

> She had nowhere to go. She climbed on the veranda and peered into Mandir. With his mace raised in his hand the Hanuman was ready to defend her! She entered the Mandir. She hugged the idol fervently and felt relieved. (p. 176).

This, however, does not bring an end to her misery. For she is spotted inside the Mandir by Rahim Khan with "a murderous look". Her son, Abdul, however, rescues her, only after inflicting grievous bodily harm on his father, Rahim Khan:

> Abdul fell upon Rahim Khan and sunk his teeth into his hand. Though Rahim Khan groaned, trying to free his hand from Abdul's mouth, he firmly held on to Shakilabanu's shoulder. As he tried freeing his own hand a strip of skin peeled off from the spot where Abdul had sunk his teeth. (p. 177)

In sum, this Muslim family's way of life is downright macabre and morbid. Shakilabanu is the worst affected victim. The inhuman treatment meted out to her prompts her to almost abandon her Islamic faith and to turn to the Hindu idol for deriving strength and security. A Muslim woman recanting her faith at the earliest opportunity available to her has been part of the tradition of Western literary Orientalism. Its earliest instance may be traced back to the twelfth century French oral poetry of the Latin European Christendom – *Chanson de Geste*. In at least twenty of these *Songs* the Muslim female is shown converting readily to Christianity. Christian knights routinely rescue her from her family tyranny. Being true to tradition, both Massinger's *Renegado* and Dryden's *Don Sebastian* have a Muslim heroine who forsakes Islam and embraces Christianity. Same holds true of the Oriental heroines in Thomas Moore's *Lalla Rookh*.[5]

Jameelakka in Kannada writer Fakir Muhammed Katpadi's "Nombu"[6] (1987) undergoes the same ordeal. Her husband's greed for dowry is insatiable. He is seen issuing dire warnings to her in an authoritarian manner. The scene reiterates the image of the tyrannical, heartless Muslim male, bent upon having his way, without any regard for norms of civility:

> Do as I say! If you utter one word in opposition I shall smash your thigh. (p. 251)

Jameelakka's feeble protest brings into sharper light the enormity of his greed:

> How much money do you want me to squeeze out of Appa? How can we manage if you don't earn anything? How much more can Appa shell out? (p.251)

His constant harassment forces his innocent wife to attempt committing suicide. Her mother and other women in neighbourhood somehow rescue her. They sympathise with her. However, they are too weak to take any action against injustice. The only consolation offered by them are some fatalistic and cynical utterances:

> Addu's mother was gently passing her hand over Jameela's head. She said, "No matter where they are, women have

> the same fate… they have to endure everything." The truth is that women should not be born on this earth…" Amma said with a sigh, then turning to Jameela, "Jameela, I have plenty of work to do. We have to live somehow till we die on this earth." (p. 257)

The brutality let loose on Jameela emaciates her, both physically and symbolically: "Jameela looked forlorn … Her face looked bleached, the eyes sunken. Her lips were dry." (p. 257)

Shaukat Osman's (b. 1917) "Alefa"[7] (Bangla, 1981) draws attention to the plight of a widow and her young daughter, ostracized as outcasts by the community. The young Alefa, like Talat in V.L. Iyengar's "Library Girl", would love to pursue studies. The morally degenerate, sex-starved and callous Muslim youths of her neighbourhood, however, deny her even such basic freedom. True to type, Muslim society is perceived as reeking of repression, stagnation and corruption:

> Alefa, who put on a burqa to go to school, had to walk ten yards though a narrow alleyway before she got on to the main road. She felt as if ten or twelve people were buried along the alleyway and she was slaking over them, while bony hands stretched out toward her. The local lads whistled at her, hung about like frustrated lovers, bringing up sighs as she passed them … Some of these lovers sang obscenities one would not expect … One day Alefa told her mother that she would much rather go to the house of Yama [the bearer of death in Hindu mythology] than to school (p. 262).

Her mother, Malika Begum, though a widow, displays some resilience and resoluteness in bringing up Alefa and in trying to get her married to a decent boy, with a good financial standing. However, the irrational, jealous and quarrelsome Muslim males of the locality humiliate the bridegroom's party on the wedding day, forcing them to leave without solemnizing marriage. It leaves both the mother and daughter shattered and rudderless. While the two shell-shocked women lay unconscious,

> A feast-mad crowd waited in the field. There was no wedding but that was no reason to starve. (p. 270)

"Alefa" thus ranks as another macabre account of Muslim life, especially the plight of Muslim woman.

Nelluri Kesavaswamy's (1920-1984) "Deliverance"[8] (Telugu, 1981) highlights the sexual exploitation of Muslim woman in the setting of a Nawab's *haveli* in the early twentieth century aristocratic Hyderabad, Deccan. The powerful Muslim male having sexual orgy in his harem with countless wives and concubines has been a recurrent spectacle in literary Orientalism. Kesavaswamy focusses, nonetheless, on the degradation inflicted upon helpless female slaves. Begum Shahi Sultan, the young Nawab's mother, forcibly sends her slave girl, Shireen, to Sultan's bedroom. Being an enlightened, educated person, Sultan does not take advantage of the helpless Shireen. He had witnessed earlier how his elder brother Siraj had sexually abused another slave girl, Jugnoo and then dumped her. His naïve plea to his mother to get his brother Siraj married with Jugnoo falls on her deaf ears. Rather, his moralistic plea enrages her:

> What? Siraj's marriage with Jugnoo ... Are you out of your mind? A servant-girl, a slave who lies beside our shoes, my son's marriage with such a woman? (p. 275)

Outraged, the Begum Sahiba fires Jugnoo whereas "Siraj Bhai went around as merrily as ever". Outside the haveli Jugnoo faces the same exploitation, which enervates her. The following portrait of hers consists of all the ingredients of the stereotype about Muslim woman – her subjugation, her helplessness and her being a victim of lust and injustice. Neither inside nor outside the Nawab's *haveli* her honour and dignity evoke any respect. She is mercilessly stripped of her identity:

> Six months later, Sultan spotted a woman who looked like Jugnoo. He was baffled. Was it she? Of course. But she had changed completely. The old robustness, the dignity, agility was missing. As though sucked dry, she had atrophied. She looked like a living corpse, without

> any glow on her face. There was no sparkle in her eyes. (pp. 275-76)

The Nawab's *haveli* retains all the features of the stereotypical "harem". As a den of vices, it houses sexually degenerate males – Siraj who exploits the slave girl Jugnoo; Shaukat, his brother-in-law who joins him in abusing Jugnoo and boasts of his sexual and moral transgressions before Sultan; the Begum Sultan; Sultan's mother, who actively encourages her sons to indulge in sexual debauchery. The only redeeming feature in Kesavaswamy's story, nonetheless, is that Sultan rises in revolt against the corrupt practices of the *haveli.* He marries the slave girl, Shireen and leads an independent life, far away from the seedy environs of the *haveli.* Notwithstanding the deliverance accomplished by Sultan, the story repeats stereotypes about Muslim way of life, particularly the misery of Muslim women.

Mohammed Khadeer Babu's (b. 1972) "Dawat"[9] (Telugu, 1981) indicts Muslim social life from the vantage point of the exploitation and extortion of the bride's parents in marriage. The main victim, nonetheless, is always the Muslim bride who faces humiliation, rather trauma for no fault of her. Left to the mercy of her in-laws, she undergoes physical and psychological torture. Often does the greed of her in-laws, culminate in her killing, euphemistically reported as "dowry death".

However, "Dawat" does not delve into such gory details. Rather, it restricts itself to pointing to the growing trend among Muslim boys for demanding huge dowry:

> They did not have enough work and did not earn much. Even then, when it came to marriage, they were demanding one lakh each … Between then and now, there had been no change in the life style of the Muslims, but the amount of dowry had increased. (p. 322)

Not unsurprisingly: "Scores of girls remains unmarried languishing in their homes" (p. 323). The exploitation of the bride's family is brought out in the story with reference to the arrival of the large number of the bridegroom's family members and friends at the bride's house for enjoying a free meal. Women being weak and inferior get a raw deal even at the festive wedding party. For they can eat only after all the men have finished eating (p. 318). Since the guests had come unannounced and in large numbers, no food was left for women. Some of the guests even staged a walk out, as a protest against the insult to them. There was commotion and chaos all over the place. Unable to maintain his poise, Aslam, the bride's uncle, exclaims in sheer disgust and desperation:

> You wretched fellows, Allah has not given me girl children. If he had, I would rather have killed them than perform such weddings for them. Why should there be so much fuss if a man and woman have to live together and lead a married life? Why so many problems? Why so much of expenditure? Why so many hundreds of people? (p. 325)

The questions posed by Aslam touch the raw nerve of Indian Muslim community. These ignoble practices – exorbitant dowry, ostentation and expenditure beyond one's means have no sanction in Islam. Worse, these social customs have made the lives of Muslim women all the more miserable, a theme permeating all the above stories. Significantly enough, most of these stories are composed by Muslim writers.

Notes and References

1. Iyengar, Vishwapriya L. "The Library Girl" (English), in *Image and Representation: Stories of Muslim Lives in India*, New Delhi, edited by Mushirul Hasan and M. Asaduddin (New Delhi, Oxford University Press, 2000), pp. 290-296.

2. Originally written in Telugu and published first in 1997, it features in *Image and Representation: Stories of Muslim Lives in India*, pp. 326-331.

3. *Image and Representation: Stories of Muslim Lives in India*: edited by Mushirul Hasan and M. Asaduddin.

4. Originally published in Gujarati in 1996, it is included in *Image and Representation*, pp. 169-179

5. For a detailed critique of Western literary Orientalism the following titles may be studied with much profit

   · Butler, Marilyn, "Orientalism" in *the Penguin History of Literature* ed. David B. Pirie. London, 1990.

   · Chew, Samuel C., *The Crescent and the Rose: Islam and England during the Renaissance*, New York, 1937.

   · Conant, Martha P., *The Oriental Tale in England in the Eighteenth Century*, New York, 1908.

   · Jafri, Naqi Husain, "Image of the Orient in Shakespeare", *Aligarh Critical Miscellany*, 11:1 (1998), 15-29.

   · Jones, C.M., "The Conventional Saracens of the *Songs of Geste*", *Speculum* 17(1942), 201-225.

   · Kabbani, Rana, *Europe's Myths of* Orient. Bloomington, 1986

   · Kahf, Mohja, Representation *of the Muslim Woman: From Termagant to Odalisque*, Austin, TX, 1999.

   · Kidwai, A.R., *Orientalism in Lord Byron's Turkish Tales*, Lewiston, USA, 1995.

- __________, (ed.), *Stranger than Fiction: Images of Islam and Muslims in English Fiction*, New Delhi, APH, 2000.
- Oueijan, Naji B., *The Progress of An Image: The East in English Literature*, New York, 1996.
- Sharafuddin, Muhammad, *Islam and Romantic Orientalism*, London, 1994.
- Smith, B.P., *Islam in English Literature*, New York, 1977.
- Said, Edward, *Orientalism*, New York, 1978.
- Wann, Louis, "The Oriental in Elizabethan Drama", *Modern Philology* 12(1915), 163-187.
- Watson, J.R., "Orientalism" in *A Handbook to English Romanticism*, eds. J. Raimond and J.R. Watson, London, 1992.

6. Published first in 1987 in Kannada, it is included in *Image and Representation*, op. cit., pp. 245-260.
7. Published first in 1981 in Bangla, it is included in *Image and Representation*, op. cit. pp. 261-270.
8. Published first in 1981 in Telugu, it is included in *Image and Representation*, op. cit. pp. 271-281.
9. Published first in 1981 in Telugu, it is included in *Image and Representation*, op. cit. pp. 317-325.

Chapter - 3

Imagining Another Pakistan – Muqaddastan: Perception of Muslims in Balwant Gargi's *Purple Moonlight*

A.R. Kidwai

Born in the undivided Punjab in 1916, Balwant Gargi did his MA in Lahore and "moved to Delhi through a blood-bath" in 1947. He made a mark as a playwright and won many prestigious national and international awards for his works. He is widely acclaimed as a distinguished writer and film maker and an authority on both classical and folk drama. His autobiographical work *Purple Moonlight* (1993)[1] touches on the lives of Muslims in India – both men and women, representing almost all the sections of society. At the one end of the scale is the affluent, highly sophisticated Begum Zaidi, standing out above others for her courtly grace and astounding knowledge of the arts, and period literature and language. At the other end is the community *mirasan* (singer) who conducts the ritual of *siapa* (mourning) in a weird manner, asking the women mourners to strip off their blouses for joining a symphony of wails, groans, shrieks and gibbers. Nonetheless, Gargi's most intriguing (mis) perception about Muslims is his imagining their aspiration for carving out another Pakistan. The observation comes out in the context of the discussion on the then raging demand for Khalistan by Sikhs:

> I tell you, Khalistan may become a reality in another fifteen years. And then there might be a demand from Muslims for Muqaddastan … the land of the holy. It may sound idiotic … Muslims may claim areas of their religious and historical glory. Ajmer Sharif, Nizamuddin Aulia, Red Fort, Jama Masjid, Taj Mahal … Fatehpur Sikri … Meerut …

> Moradabad ... Faizabad ... Imambaras of Lucknow ... their heritage. Do you realise? Muslims feel that they have been crushed under the majority rule of Hindus for the past forty years. They are sixteen percent of the population but their voice in the government and military is hardly four percent ... After twenty years Muslims will swell to three hundred millions, fives times that of France ... seven times of England ... thirty times of Saudi Arabia ... and if they demand a separate State, we should not be shocked. Perhaps in twenty years there will be a Muqaddastan![2]

Gargi's perception of Muslims in this instance is marked by ambivalence. On the one hand, it is alarmist, alerting the Hindu majority community in particular and other faith communities in India to the ominous, though highly inflated, menace of the rapidly growing Muslim population in India, which is bound to change irrevocably the present demography soon. On the other, Muslims' marginalization in public life is also acknowledged. Implicit in it is the warning that the sense of injustice and discrimination as perceived by Muslims coupled with their ever-growing numbers, will lead them on to the path of separation, resulting in another Partition. Equally disturbing is the suggestion that soon after forming a sizeable part of population, Muslims would be quick to reclaim their lost glory, wresting power and territory from Hindus. The choice of place name in this context is highly emotive. "Muqaddastan", a mix of Arabic and Persian words, is defined by Gargi as "the land of the holy", which rhymes both literally and metaphorically with Pakistan. For Pakistan literally means "the land of the pure". The Muslim psyche, as portrayed by Gargi, appears as menacing and deranged. For, "Muslims feel that they have been *crushed under the majority rule of Hindu*" (italics added). Throughout the description Muslims are referred to as "they", up in arms against "we" – the Indians. It is worth-clarifying that Gargi's reference is not to the on-going separatist militancy in Kashmir. Rather, he ascribes blatant separatism to the mainland Muslims of India. Such an alarmist view of Muslim presence is otherwise uncommon in the mainstream Indian writings in English.

Being a victim of the Partition of the country in 1947 reducing him to a refugee, Gargi inevitably refers first to the catastrophic event which left an indelible mark on his life in his formative years. He relates with abhorrence the brutality let loose in the wake of the event. What baffles him most is the abuse of religion in perpetrating inhuman acts by all the faith communities. By coincidence, as a refugee he gets the lodging in Delhi which was occupied earlier by the employees of a Muslim nawab. Gargi nonetheless speaks of them as having "fled to Pakistan"[3] whereas he had "moved" to Delhi.

His glowing tribute to the Urdu poet philosopher, Muhammad Iqbal (d. 1938) is characterized by streaks of ambivalence: His observations are occasioned by his argument with Ali Sardar Jafri who earned notoriety for Iqbal-bashing. He silences the latter, telling him plainly:

> But Iqbal is great ... I am not a Muslim. I don't believe in Allah or Satan or Karbala or Hejaz. Why does Iqbal move me? Something enters my blood ... brings tears to my eyes ... when he describes the power of Muslims ... the flashing sword of Islam ... their conquests ... I am moved to the depth of my soul."[4]

Read together with Gargi's above-quoted passage on Muslims' imaginary demand for a separate state carved out of India – Muqaddastan, the tribute to Iqbal's poetry immediately brings to mind "the flashing sword of Islam", with its dark shadows over India. Islam, in Gargi's mind, stands only for "conquests" and he notes its reflection in Iqbal's poetical works.

Contrary to Gargi's assertion, Iqbal's poetry is not so jingoistic. As pointed out by an eminent Iqbal critic, Asloob Ahmad Ansari,

> Iqbal's claims to greatness rest on his value system being important in and for itself – and this value system may be characterized as rational, vitalistic and forward-looking – as also on the fact that he has been able to provide for this value-system intellectual coherence, emotional depth and poetic force ... He has articulated through his poetry the

> anxiety and aspirations, the sense of fulfilment as well as the frustration of the contemporary man with a rare degree of honesty and perspicacity.[5]

Gargi's fascination for Laila, a beautiful Muslim Iraqi woman whom he met by chance in Russia, is reminiscent of the Western literary Orientalists' fondness for the exotic. It is not therefore, sheer co-incidence that Laila's charming beauty transports his mind to the *Arabian Nights*. The ethereal Oriental beauty, referred to as the "siren"[6] by Gargi, disappears as abruptly as she had made her appearance. She does not seem to have any reality. To the same exotic, unreal category belongs another Muslim woman, the princely Begum Qudsia Zaidi:

> She smoked an expensive hookah with a sliver wired *chillam* and a winding silver-tipped pipe, and chewed betel-leaves of the choicest variety out of a filigreed box which her page carried around ... Her courtly grace and feminine charm mesmerized people. She commanded, and the highest submitted."[7]

It is worth-noting that the association of Muslims with the exotic underscores their marginal existence.

Another feature of Western literary Orientalism of identifying Muslim male with sexual debauchery, enjoying his harem, is to the fore also in Gargi's account of his friend, Habịb Tanvir, a young theatre director from Delhi:

> Habib was known as a lady killer in those days. Women could not resist his charms ... Like the hero of Chekhov's Don Jaun in Russian Style, Habib had become a target of women's love [in Russia] and was on the verge of collapse. He did not know what to do with this she-demon who came to his bed every night slobbering all over him.[8]

Imroz, another Muslim male, is not, however, so fortunate as to be flanked all the time by beautiful women. Rather, he is depicted as an irrational person and as a jealous, possessive and authoritarian husband. In sum, he typifies a common stereotype about Muslim male. His wife, Amrita Pritam is seen complaining bitterly against him: "That fellow … that Imroz … jealous and possessive … he reduced me to a domestic drudge.[9] Derogatory epithets such as "cruel and impossible" and "jealous"[10] are lavishly heaped on him.

Far worse is the description of another Muslim – a thief who breaks into Gargi's house and is caught red-handed: "A puny man in a chequered *lungi* and tattered shirt crouched in a corner." His plea for pardon in chaste Urdu interspersed with Islamic terminology unmistakably establishes his Muslim identity:

> The man was trembling. He slowly got up and folded his hands, "Pardon me huzoor. Have mercy on me. May Allah –".[11]

His dehumanization reaches its crescendo, as he is equated with a repulsive rat:

> Tara Singh tore a piece of fish and tossed it to him. "Eat it, rat. We share our food even with thieves."
> The thief caught the tossed fish in both hands, raised it to his forehead and started nibbling it.[12]

Muslim masses appear as a lot that conjures up images of their being dated, chaotic, dirty and poor. When Gargi takes Hollywood director, Elia Kazan and his wife, Barbara to Jama Masjid, Delhi, they are haunted by such scenes:

> We walked around the mosque and down the jewellery bazar. Merchants reclined … amidst their primitive weighing scales and ornaments … We walked down the steps into a lane thickly populated with Muslim shops of the old world. Steaming biryani, cauldrons of meat bubbling on flaming ovens, smoke-filled dingy shops. Hefty butchers hacking at hunks of the choicest meats. Women in black burqas sitting like huge cats on cycle rickshaws,

> their eyes blinking from behind squares of gauze. Beggars hobbling on crutches, seeking alms in the name of Allah.[13]

From this generalization there is a move towards particularization. Reshma, a gypsy singer from Pakistan, an artist in her own right, reeks of sheer vulgarity, greed and ill manners.

> She was a mix of ignorance and cunning and repeated stories of her life at every *mehfil*. People listened to these and laughed because she made them juicy by her mannerism. She said to me: "This shawl, woven in gold thread, was presented to me by the President of the Urdu Conference ..."
>
> But the organizers told me that Reshma had extracted it ... She had also taken a large sum in cash.
>
> A stream of filth flowed from that throat which poured out songs of beauty, love and yearnings ... That throat had turned into a sewer. A river of mud.[14]

In sum, apart from containing valuable insights into literary history, and contemporary politics and arts, Gargi's autobiographical work makes some disturbing statements about the Muslim presence in India. Notwithstanding his liberal outlook on life and happenings, Gargi's account of Muslims regrettably retains some of the stereotypes conventionally featuring in Western literary Orientalism.

Notes and References

1. Balwant Gargi, *Purple Moonlight*, Delhi, UBSPD, 1994, The first edition came out in 1993. All textual references are to 1994 edition.
2. Ibid., p. 177.
3. Ibid., p. 2
4. Ibid., p. 7
5. Asloob Ahmad Ansari, "Iqbal as Poet and Thinker", *Iqbal Review* (1970), p. 132
6. *Purple Moonlight*, p. 40
7. Ibid., p. 67
8. Ibid., pp. 36 and 37
9. Ibid., p. 74
10. Ibid., p. 75
11. Ibid., p. 82
12. Ibid., p. 82
13. Ibid., p. 111
14. Ibid., pp. 132 and 135

Chapter - 4

The Trope of Home and the Representation of Muslim Women in Rokeya Sakhawat Hossain and in Attia Hosain's *Sunlight on a Broken Column*

Md. Mahmudul Hasan

Abstract: The trope of home has received a perennial interest in both the writings of colonialist writers and in the works of those from colonised society. Whereas the colonialists are keen on expanding their "home" in foreign territories, the colonised remain culturally dislocated in their own homeland and engage in ideological debates to regain it. In the patriarchal discourse, women are relegated to the private world of home and family. In recent feminist theory, women, especially from subaltern societies, seek for a space to have a sense of belonging. The issue of multiple meanings of home and of multiple modes of homelessness finds symbolic representation in Rokeya's feminist works and in Attia's *Sunlight on a Broken Column* (1961). In the light of their treatment of the trope of home, this paper touches upon its re-readings in the feminist ideology of "being home and non-being home"(Martin & Mohanty, 1988, p.196). Occasional references are made to Woolf's *A Room of One's Own* (1929), which also deals with women's longing for home and for belongingness. I propose to subvert the binarism of private and public, and of male and female associated with the received notion of the home. The homelessness of the colonised because of colonial dispossession, and women's homeless condition because of their gender orientation constitute the central thesis of this paper. Whereas the gendered, domestic norms of *izzat* (honour) and *sharum* (modesty) restrict women's independence and impede their individual fulfilment, colonial structures and education policy render the colonised culturally dislocated and spiritually homeless. In this regard, I endorse Sahgal's (1993) assertion that "[...] migration can take place without even leaving one's soil" (p.119). Even after the decolonisation, the legacy of the colonial cultural and education policy continues to culturally displace indigenous peoples. It has created an ambivalence among the colonised of adopting western value systems (especially "individualism") and preserving their cultural rootedness. This difficult predicament is a palpable consequence of colonialism.]

The issue of home is of lasting significance in world literatures. Expanding the home-space by the colonisers at the expense of the loss of it for the colonised made it a generic subject matter in the writings of both colonialist writers, and in those of the writers from colonised lands as well as diasporic writers. Whereas "the novel of the Empire" characteristically concerns itself with the "adventures of the open spaces" (Kaul & Jain, 2001, p.141) and of unconquered lands, the feminist anti-colonial novel explores the internal home-space for the warmth of human relationship and for a shared place for both men and women. In recent critical discourses, 'home' gets an eclectic attention. The concern for the location where the self can feel "at home", the search for home, the discovery of home and the "return to home" permeate political, ethnic and nationalist, cultural and feminist studies. More precisely, the issue of linking up the self to an emotionally comfortable location has been a primary project of modern literature.

Given the fact that "there is a great deal of regional variation in social structure, values and customs and problems in different parts of India" (Mukherjee, 1971, p.26), there are not many generic themes in the works of Indian writers from different regions. But "home" is one of the predominant themes, as women's *not being home* and the colonial dispossession of indigenous peoples from their home are common experiences in all Indian regions. A shared sense of homelessness was lurking in the consciousness of the writers of that time, as they were desperate to find a place which they could call their home. So, no matter that Rokeya wrote from Calcutta, and Attia lived in Lucknow and then migrated to Britain where she wrote most of her works, a longing for home and a sense of rootlessness runs through their writings. Rokeya's and Attia's treatment of loss and nostalgia is diametrically opposed to the male nationalist perception, which is primarily concerned about certain interests and agendas that relegate women to a privatised domestic sphere and exclude them from the public domain. In opposition to this hegemonic, patriarchal view of women's space in the home and in nation, Rokeya's and Attia's feminist view challenges the classical distinction between the public and the private. In *Sunlight on a Broken Column*, Attia represents the disintegration of the home and the troubled period of the Partition through the consciousness of a young Muslim woman, Laila, whose reading of the events carries its own feminist value judgements.

Rokeya's and Attia's personal experiences about homelife are divergent to some extent. For Rokeya home was everything in her early life; she was secretly educated by her elder brother at home and was never trained in any institution outside her domestic setting. Rokeya's homelife can be compared with that of Jane Austen who had to cover "her manuscripts" with a "piece of blotting-paper" (Woolf, 1929, p.61). The metaphor of "attic" has a concrete relevance to Rokeya's life. Rokeya (1931b) recounts her own internment in an attic in the following way:

> Once, when I was five, I was staying in Calcutta in the residence of my second sister-in-law's aunt's residence. Two maidservants from Bihar came to see my sister-in-law; they had 'free passport' to walk around the home. For the fear of life, I had to hide myself here and there like a fawn – sometimes behind a door-panel or under a table. There was a desolate attic on the third floor. The aunt used to take me up in her arms and keep me there, where I had to stay and nothing was there to eat almost the whole day. (p.387)

Rokeya's female psyche during the formative period of her life was closer to Gilbert's and Gubar's representation of women in their *The Madwoman in the Attic*. Conversely, Attia enjoyed the opportunity of having an English governess for her education at home. She studied outside her domestic environment, first at the elite La Martiniere School and, later, at the Isabella Thoburn College in Lucknow. Attia had the honour of being the first woman from the feudalistic Taluqdar family to graduate from Lucknow University. Moreover, in Attia's family tradition, women's education and 'voyage out' were not unprecedented. Her mother Nisar Fatima received home education in Arabic, Persian and Urdu. Nisar's younger sister Inam Fatima, a social worker and Muslim League activist, "wrote a travel journal *Safar-e-Europe* [Travel to Europe] about her trip to England in 1924" and "was elected to the UP Legislative Assembly in 1937" (Shamsie, 2004). A similar 'voyage out' for Rokeya was next to impossible. She had to resort to her imagination to come out of the home through her feminist utopia *Sultana's Dream*. This divergence in their experiences was because of the time as well as the place to which they belonged.

Rokeya wrote in the early twentieth-century, when a popular movement for an independent India from the colonial rule was gaining ground. So an all-pervasive emotional experience of the loss of the homeland and of the struggle to regain it, and the search for one's identity find an eloquent expression in her writings. But what is special in her treatment of home is that, she links women's marginality in their own home with the homelessness of men in their own country. Attia also registers women's peripheralised condition in the home through the very autobiographical nature of her novel *Sunlight on a Broken Column*.

Born in India in a respectable Kidwai Taluqdari family of Lucknow, Attia Hosain moved to Britain in "1946 when [her] husband [...] was posted to the Indian High Commission" in London (Bhuchar, 1998, p.43). She stayed on in the metropole after the independence and the Partition of India; hence she belongs to the early period of the formation of an Asian diaspora in Britain. Attia experienced homelessness from dual perspectives: her experiences with colonial culture in India, and her exilic life in London later on. Being one of the early immigrants, emotionally Attia had the whole brunt of the anguish of a diasporic life, as she states, "My background made me belong to a class that does not, and never has, taken me into itself" (quoted in Shamsie, 2004); and "what it means being here then and what it means here, being an Asian, now are two different things" (quoted in Bhuchar, 1998, p.44). Attia's ambivalences between India where she grew up, and Britain, her adopted home, remain irreconcilable. So her writing and broadcasting with the BBC, and her involvement with the world of theatre and the arts were attempts on her part to create a world of her own and to capture the phantom of her lost home that is India. Her self-exilic and diasporic condition can be compared with Edward Said's dislocated past and denial of identities as a Palestinian living in the West, as it finds a symbolic representation in his *After the Last Sky* (1986), a prototypical work that articulates the features of the émigré genre. Like Said, Attia faced the same ordeal of not being able to "belong exclusively to one country" (Said, 1991, p.116). In fact, this caught-between-two-worlds status is not exclusively a condition of exile. Attia, like many of her colonised compatriots, experienced the same situation of in-betweenness while in India, as Anand (1978) observes, "And the alienation caused by her schooling in English language, had made her grow up between the proverbial two worlds, the one not quite yet dead and the other refusing to be born" (p.4). Nadira in *SBC* touches upon the same ambivalence when she remarks that, she along with Laila and the like "are paying for being the product of two cultures [...]" (p.211). Actually, Attia's homelessness while in India was a direct result of the cultural dislocation caused by colonial education policies in India. I will take up this issue of cultural rootlessness later in this essay.

Attia's alienation both in India and in Britain has more to do with her "loss of an identity [. . .] a wrenching away from all things dear and familiar – family, home, language, country" (Kaul & Jain, 2001, p.112), a world she knew. Her essential homelessness and her longing for home are largely represented in her portrayal of Laila in *SBC*, a novel that typifies émigré literature. Like her creator, Laila also suffers from her situatedness in two worlds: one is her domestic life, and the other is her life in the outer world. She is sandwiched between the traditional values and mores of her home life, and the exclusionary, masculinist outside world. Laila voices:

> I used to forget that the world was in reality very different, and the voices that controlled it had once been those of

> Baba Jan, Aunt Abida, Ustaniji, and now belonged to Uncle Hamid, Aunt Saira, and their friends. Always I lived in two worlds, and I grew to resent the 'real' world. (p.128)

Attia's outsiderness was caused by her migrant situation whereas Laila's strangerhood in her own homeland is caused by her gender orientation. No matter Attia was in London and Laila in Lucknow, the essential sense of unbelongingness and an intense longing for *being home* are common in both of them. Woolf (1938) passionately touches upon this universal condition of women when she states, "As a woman, I have no country. As a woman I want no country" (p.234). Woolf is particularly concerned about the relegation of women to the private world of home and about the exclusion of women from the external world, a destiny common to women in global perspective. The Partition saga reinforces the homeless condition of Indian women. During the communal riots and the mass massacre of the Paritition, many women were subjected to abduction and forced marriage with men from their "enemy" community. After a few years when both the Governments of India and the newly created Pakistan had an agreement to return those women to their families, women were not easily accepted. In this regard, Butalia (1998) points towards a difference in the attitude of Muslims and Hindus in accepting their women back: "Apparently, abducted Muslim women were more easily accepted back into their families" (p.161). Among Hindus and Sikhs, the concept of purity was stronger, hence Hindu and Sikh women's reinstatement in their family was tougher. By sleeping with men of 'other' community, women supposedly lost their 'purity' and acted beyond the premise of *izzat* and *sharum*. Thus women's belonging to their family and home is defined by scores of social customs and mythologies, whereas men enjoy an assured sense of belonging.

Laila in *SBC* struggles against her class and social conditioning, and is in the search for a home to belong to. An acute nostalgic sense and an urge to return to her roots haunt her throughout the novel. On her visit to Lucknow fourteen years after the Partition, Laila notices that the "town has changed beyond recognition – arches, domes, the mall, almost everything" (Kidwai, 2005, p.63). The same feeling of loss grips her when she revisits her ancestral home Ashiana (the nest): "Patches of damp and peeling plaster disfigured the house like the skin of a once beautiful woman struck by leprosy" (*SBC*, p.271). While the *SBC* is Attia's nostalgic commemoration of home, Ashiana brings Laila back to her past and reminds her of her present homelessness. Upon her entering Ashiana, now in a deserted condition, fragments of her past burst through her present. Through the character portrayal of Laila, Attia actually tries to divulge her own sense of longing for home, which is also a predominant theme of her collection of short stories *Phoenix Fled*. Muneeza Shamsie (2004) terms Attia's *Phoenix Fled* as an attempt on her part to recapture "the India she had left behind". Away from home, Attia remained true to her Indian identity and cultural heritage; hence we notice a sensibility of an exile, a constant to-and-fro-movement between the past and the present in the novel *SBC*.

Though Rokeya did not migrate to any foreign country, she could not escape the fate of being homeless. As it is a common destiny for all women in traditional Indian society, Rokeya had to leave her natal home for the marital household in Bhagalpur[1]. After her husband's death, she had to leave Bhagalpur because of the ill-treatment she received from some of her in-laws. Rokeya finally moved to Calcutta. Although Rokeya remained within her own country and was shrouded by her own culture, she also feels dislocated, as if she was in a foreign land. An acute sense of homelessness and of nostalgia is transmitted in many of her letters she wrote to her relatives and colleagues about her life in Calcutta. The following letter she wrote to one Mr. Yasin sharply describes the anguish of her exilic life in Calcutta:

> You need not feel so keenly about me, I do not repent for leaving Bhagalpur, but at times I feel some sort of yearning to see the grave of my husband and the tiny graves of my babies. But never mind. I am brave enough to bear my grief. (Rokeya, 1913, p. 504).

Both Rokeya's and Attia's dislocation disrupted their lives and destroyed their earlier support structures. This fatality is common to any exilic situation. It is like a transplanted plant that requires massive efforts for cultivation in the new soil. A strong sense of outsiderness and of fringe dwelling runs through the writings of Rokeya and Attia, for their being women writers and for their essential diasporic situation.

Rokeya had, among other things, two agendas before her: to struggle for the regaining of her homeland from the colonisers, and to give women a space to feel at home in her culture. In the context of colonial dispossession by the British in India, Rokeya examines the state of her homeless community vis-à-vis the condition of women. According to Rokeya, the colonial condition of belonging and unbelonging, place and displacement, territorialization and deterritorialization is closely linked with the condition of women in her society. She articulates the notion of the home through the ideological determinant of gender. Rokeya relates the issue of reclaiming the colonised homeland to the independence of women from domestic incarceration. Similarly, in *Sunlight on a Broken Column*, two struggles go along side each other: struggle for the independence of India from the colonial grip; and Laila's struggles to free herself from the shackles of patriarchal familial cords, her longing for freedom and for agency.

Rokeya is a visionary in her demand for liberating women from domestic seclusion. She wants men to free women so that they can take part in activities outside the home; at the same time, she does not undermine the potentially enabling and enhancing activities of the home. To be more precise, Rokeya urges men to end their authoritarian rule in the home in order that women can have a congenial home-life free from patriarchal oppression. Conversely, she directs women to do their best to turn their domestic space into an inclusive place for men and women to live in, a place where both will receive equal treatment. Rokeya rejects the notion of confinement and harem[2] fantasies associated with the home; rather she believes in its possibilities as a source of security and stability for both men and women. Against dominant gendered concepts of home conceived by patriarchy, Rokeya provides an alternative notion that engages the debates of modern feminist struggle of reclaiming the home. She subverts the binarisms of private and public, and of male and female associated with the notion of home. Rokeya shifts away from the patriarchal definition of women's position in the home in order to enforce women's belongingness at home.

Rokeya does not exclusively relate women's emancipation to their freedom from domestic condition. She states, "Do women of all societies remain confined in seclusion? Or have I called them progressive because they are not *purdanashin* (confined in seclusion)? I basically talked about their 'enslaved' mind" (Rokeya, 1904, p.25). She hints at the fact that by just living outside seclusion women do not become liberated. True liberation comes when they make the best of their private and public spheres; and this will happen only when women earn a strong sense of belonging in both the worlds. Through the character of Zahra, Attia shows how women's just crossing out of the domestic thresholds does not suggest their liberation. Before her marriage with Naseer, she was perfectly "a dutiful purdah girl". Soon after her marriage, she seems to have earned some liberty and starts attending "social functions morning, afternoon and evening". Despite her supposed "mannerisms" and "sophistication", Laila casts doubt on her actual aptitude to live a truly liberated life: "I knew she had not changed within herself. She was now playing the part of the perfect modern wife as she had once played the part of a dutiful purdah girl" (p.140). Like Woolf's (1938) construction of women's conscious "earned money influence" (p.152), Rokeya and Attia want women to earn their conscious liberty and to use it productively.

Like Rokeya, Virginia Woolf (1938) also points towards women's responsibility to enhance their new home, to beautify it as an inclusive place, as she puts, "Light up the windows of the new house, daughters! Let them blaze!" (p. 208). Woolf (1929) rejects the binarism of private and public, associated with the notion of home, as she puts, "[…] I thought how unpleasant it is to be locked out; and I thought how it is worse perhaps to be locked in […]" (p.21). Like Rokeya, Woolf also does not think that by just freeing women from domestic incarceration, their equitable share in society can be established. In Rokeya and Woolf, both private and public worlds are intertwined. Women have to have a comfortable existence or homelife in both the worlds, as Woolf (1938) argues, "the public and the private worlds are inseparably connected [...] the tyrannies and servilities of the one are the tyrannies and servilities of the others" (p.270). What is needed is a strong sense of belonging for women within the home and without. Both Rokeya and Woolf want women, to quote Woolf (1929), "to live in the presence of reality, an invigorating life" (p.99). Similarly Attia also proposes that women should live a down-to-earth, pragmatic life. In the character of Aunt Saira, Attia provides a vivid example of a woman who does not live a realistic life. Having lived an unrealistic life, Saira knew "only the fruits of possession, not the mechanics" (*SBC*, p.276) of family, hence became totally lost when the feudalistic family structure broke down because of the Partition.

Both Rokeya and Woolf maintain their reservations about the relegation of women to the private world of home and family, which causes their social isolation and denies them direct experiences of the real world. They want to free women from the ideological burdens associated with the metaphor of "a frog in a well" (Rokeya, 1905, p.466). Through the character of Rani Sahiba in *SBC*, Attia makes a social protest against such deadening confinement of women. Once brought out from domestic confinement for her to cast vote, the Rani (Queen) looks "a frightened animal in unfamiliar surroundings" (*SBC*, p.257); she even does not know how and who to vote, as her conversation with Laila adequately shows:

> I said slowly, "You have to vote for four out of the eight whose names are on the paper."
>
> "Vote? I do not understand. And I cannot read. Manager Sahib knows." (*SBC* p.258).

Attia represents home as an ideological battleground where contending ideas clash with each other. Laila, being "an observer in an outside world", feels "solitary" in her own private world (*SBC* p.124). In the domestic condition of Abida's marital home, Laila is looked at as "someone from another world" (*ibid.*, p.250). Home in *SBC* is multiply divided; there are many homes within the home, separated by ideological boundaries. In

Laila's world, there is one rule for men and another for women, one standard for married women and another for unmarried ones. Even though girls have limited or "controlled freedom" (*ibid.*, p.202), a married young woman enjoys a degree of advantage over a non-married one. After Zahra's marriage she receives relatively a greater freedom, as Laila states, "You are different now that you are married" (*ibid.*, p.141). A plethora of patriarchal norms were employed to restrict "an unmarried girl's freedom" (*ibid.*, p.210).

In the character of Baba Jan, who maintains a haunting presence in the consciousness of the characters in the story and readers alike (though we never meet him in the text), Attia gives a symbolic representation of the unquestioned authority of patriarchal domestic norms. In the ageing figure of Baba Jan, Attia presents a composite of the coercing power of patriarchal regulations that "reduced" the inmates of his home "to fearing automatons" (*ibid.*, p.31). Failing to abide by these value systems by a woman leads to her inevitable homelessness.

Attia shows how "a Muslim girl, from a strict purdah family" (*ibid.*, p.132) is rendered homeless and is compelled to commit suicide because of her non-compliance with the feudalistic patriarchal norms. But society's disapproval of the "boy" who equally disregards such norms is milder; he does not become homeless and is readily accepted by his family once "he yielded to pressure and abandoned the girl" (*ibid.*, p.133). This gendered discrepancy is governed by society's received notion that a woman should show "more *sharum* than a man and failure to do so risks damaging the honour of herself, her family and her caste" (Gomis, 2002, p.106). The twin concepts of *izzat* (honour) and *sharum* (modesty) are presumed to be embodied in women, whereas these values are applied in a relaxed mode to men. Family honour is "defined in relation to a woman's body and a man's authority" (Kaul & Jain, 2001, p.169). Through Laila's protest against this patriarchal ideology, Attia expresses her disapproval of such strict gendered norms. Attia herself defied "the demands of family loyalty and 'honour' (*izzat*)" (Nabar, 2000, p.123) by marrying her first cousin Ali Bahadur Habibullah (Sonny) against her mother's wishes. In *SBC*,

Laila becomes homeless for her non-compliance with *izzat* and for her marrying Ameer against the family expectations.

In order to attain her personal fulfilment, Laila adheres to western individualistic ideals. In so doing, she has to compromise with her family loyalty and, eventually, to leave her home. Her defiance against family norms terribly angers her most beloved aunt Abida, as Laila puts, "She [Aunt Abida] refused to see me or reply to my letters once I had told her I could not obey her, nor my family, and deny Ameer" (*SBC* p.312). In a fiery exchange of words Abida reprimands Laila, "You have been defiant and disobedient. You have put yourself above your duty to your family" (*ibid.*). Laila tries to reconcile her "purity of love" for Ameer with her loyalty to family. But in Indian context, such contending loyalties are un-negotiable, as it is a concrete experience for Laila in *SBC*. Laila defies family demands and marries Ameer. Her shifting loyalty from family to personal fulfilment ends her marriage with Ameer "with the blessings of not one of my [Laila's] elders" (*ibid.*).

Conversely, in Rokeya's *Padmaraga*, Lalif, an England-returned barrister, gives in to the pressures of his elders, and agrees to marry Saleha, a choice of his Uncle Habib Alam. Like Laila, Latif also encounters a difficult predicament of personal choice and family loyalty. Laila disregards family expectations; Latif surrenders to his family demands and marries Saleha. But interestingly, whereas Laila becomes homeless because of her non-compliance, Latif encounters the same destiny because of his compliance. Having Saleha as a wife at home, Latif virtually loses his homelife in the home and becomes a spiritual vagabond, who hunts for emotional comfort and for homelife away from his domestic circumstances. After his marriage with Saleha, Latif cannot stay at his home for more than six months. He has to stay away from his home most of the time. Though sometimes he comes home, he never finds the comfort he expects from Saleha; there has always been a void in his heart, his psyche has always remained *asroihin* (shelterless) even though at times he appears physically to be at home (p.288). Thus, given the concrete experiences of Laila and Latif, it can be correctly argued that the traditional Indian family norms of unquestioned family loyalty can potentially render a person, man or woman, homeless if they pursue personal fulfilment in opposition to family demands. And in this case, I endorse Vrinda Nabar's (2000) assertion that in the Indian context, "constraint[s] on individual freedom" (p.124) apply equally to both men and women. This shared destiny of man and woman is largely true when individuals' choices clash with family's in selecting spouses. But in general, it is women who have to bear the brunt of family demands and domestic regulations.

Different rules apply to the dwellers of the home on the basis of gender orientation. Men can breach the "code of feudal honour" they build with impunity, by visiting courtesans and by living a life of sexual profligacy, while they confine "their daughters in purdah or semi-purdah" (Anand, 1978, p.3). The clear division of the home between *zenana* (women's quarters) and *mardana* (men's quarters) makes it easier for men to impose their will "on the females, especially the daughters and the nieces" (Kaul & Jain (2001, p.58). Men want their women to stay in the zenana quarters and not to interact with the outside world. Nandi is beaten by her father Jumman because, to use Jumman's words, "the wretch [Nandi] was found by the driver with the cleaner in the garage" (*SBC* p.27). Nandi's whining self-defence that she "went to give him a shirt that he had forgotten" (*ibid.*) was not accepted for the obvious reason that she defies the feudalistic rule of gender segregation, and thus offends against family norms.

This home regimentation of women also works as a big hurdle against female education. Laila faces a stiff resistance in her pursuance of learning from Hakiman Bua, a senior female servant. In traditional Indian society, household maidservants are usually picked from poor relatives or from distant connections; and they are treated as second-grade family members. Many domestic servants spend their whole life in the service of the family, and their long service in return earned them some sort of authority, which they sometimes exercise to discipline the younger generation of the family. It is because of her long-service, Hakiman Bua works as a natural instrument of patriarchal will, hence she dares to remonstrate:

> Your books will eat you. They will dim the light of your lovely eyes, my moon princess, and then who will marry

> you, owl-eyed, peering through glasses? Why are you not like Zahra, your father's—God rest his soul—own sister's child, yet so different from you? Pull your head out of your books and look at the world, my child. (*SBC* p.14)

Thus, in the Indian context, female education became an antithesis of the established norms of homelife. Education for girls was looked at as a defiant challenge to the dynamics of social system, as Rokeya (1931c) puts, "Education for women has therefore become anonymous with us for breaking the barrier of ancient custom which shut them from learning" (p.481). Laila's existence within her home is constrained by various types of home norms, and is "guarded by a thousand taboos fiercer than the most fiery dragons" (*SBC*, p.191).

Throughout the novel *SBC*, Laila has to remain as a passive onlooker of the tumultuous happenings around her: the popular movement against the colonisers, the partition of the country and the consequent animosity between and the polarisation of Hindus and Muslims[3]. Whereas the male members of the family are acting as players in these upheavals, Laila, having lived "a cocooned life", has to watch "silently and passively all that happens to and around her" (Kidwai, 2005, p.60). This compulsory silence and conditioned passivity in Attia's fictional world can be compared with Butalia's real post-independence world, where Butalia notices an internalised tongue-tiedness among women who suffered the traumas of the Partition. In her recounting of women's stories, Butalia (1998) observes, "Women almost never spoke about themselves, indeed they denied they had anything 'worthwhile' to say, a stance that was often corroborated by their men. Or, quite often, they simply weren't there to speak to" (p.126).

Against the patriarchal notion of the home, both Rokeya and Attia present a utopian home space where women do not have to encounter familial and social regimentations. Rokeya's representations of the "Ladyland" in *Sultana's Dream* (1905) and of Tarini Bhaban in *Padmaraga* (1924) are two striking examples of utopian and semi-utopian homeland and domestic space. In the "Ladyland" men are conditioned to stay in domestic seclusion, and they are happy to give the franchise to women to accomplish all public activities, including statecraft and military affairs. In Tarini Bhaban, women enjoy full liberty. It is an antithesis of the social order where women are repressed by patriarchal home rules. While in the domestic condition in Indian society, women are denied any voice in their personal affairs, in Tarini Bhaban women exercise full control over their lives. In the realistic world, Zaynab had little role in the fixation of her marriage with Latif, as it was arranged by her family; but here in Tarini Bhaban, it is Zaynab who is to decide about the course of her future life. Rafiya, one of the residents of Tarini Bhaban, states, "Who can dare to marry off Siddiqa [Zaynab]? If she does not agree, nobody can force her to marry" (*Padmaraga,* p.327). In *SBC*, Laila makes a utopian "home" in the concluding section of the novel (p.307); this home is different from Baba Jan's patriarchal home that "does not welcome" her (*SBC* p.313). Under the tutelage of authoritarian male guardians, Laila has "never been allowed to make decisions; they are always made for" her (*SBC* p.265). By making her utopian home, Laila realises her dream of living her own life; and she has been "able to break from traditional customs [...]" (ibid., p.316).

Laila's first utopian home is Ameer's residence where she moved as his wife, and thus realised her personal fulfilment. On her arrival at Ameer's home Laila says, "I was happy to have a home of my very own, to live in it as I pleased without dictation, though it was small and simple, and without scores of servants as in Hasanpur and Ashiana" (*SBC* p.315). After Ameer's death, Laila makes her second utopian home, which is an all-female home where she lives with Shahla, Laila's daughter by Ameer, and with Nandi. Sita and Romana are frequent visitors to this feminist home. Laila's utopian home disregards the patriarchal notions of *izzat* and *sharum*; here Nandi remains unscathed even though she has become pregnant through extramarital sex. Nandi says to Laila:

> If I had stayed at home, even if *he* [Nandi's "old dotard" husband] had not dared, my father would have thrown

> me out. Or the old fool might have fancied his youth had returned and claimed the child, and I would have been tied to him for ever. I could not endure him any longer, and I wanted the child. So I came to you, knowing I would be safe here. (*SBC*, p.291)

Through the representation of Laila's home, Attia presents an alternative home, where women are not subject to inhibiting patriarchal measures and have control over their own life. Laila's journey from Ashiana to the hill-station where she makes her own home can be compared with Lily Briscoe's voyage from Ramsay house to the Lighthouse in Woolf's *To the Lighthouse* (1927). Through her escape from the realistic world of the Ramsays to her visionary utopian world, Lily creates a different home where she is not governed by patriarchal demands. Thus, for the realisation of a woman's fullest independence, the need for a home of her own, or "a room of her own" (Woolf, 1929, p.3), that will give her a strong sense of belonging, is strongly felt across the feminist works of Rokeya, Woolf and Attia.

Together with the homeless condition of women in the social order, Rokeya and Attia also touch upon the cultural rootlessness of both men and women in the colonised social space. They deal with the cultural displacement from home, in other words, homelessness within the home, which has been an essential colonial condition. In the discussion that follows, I will endorse the following two assertions:

> [...] migration can take place without even leaving one's soil. Where does one culture begin and another end when they are housed in the same person? (Sahgal, 1993, p.119).

> Home is also the imagined location that can be more readily fixed in a mental landscape than in actual geography. (George, 1996, p.11)

According to Sahgal and George, being home and not being home have the undercurrent meaning of belonging and estrangement, not merely residing in any geographical location or out of it. They emphasise the cultural formulations of the concept of home. Home is a sign of difference and is deeply involved in the politics of inclusion and exclusion. A careful look at Rokeya's and Attia's works will establish these contentions. In their views, homelessness or migration is not something peculiar to leaving one's native land; it can happen in one's one home, or land.

In Rokeya's *Gyanphal*, the females of Kanaka Dipa (the isle of gold) have made an affinity with the [English] fairies, and started to imitate their outfits and ornaments. What was left was copying their wings (Rokeya, 1922, p.136). Rokeya points towards this cultural mimicry, and demonstrates it as one of the reasons for losing their country to the English fairies (the colonisers). In "Nurse Nelly", she relates Noyeema's homelessness to her alienation from her own culture, which forces her out of her home. In Noyeema's character, Rokeya exposes one consequence of women's domestic incarceration and of keeping them away from the light of education and intellectual exercise. Having lived her life in women's private sphere of stagnation and intellectual dereliction (except for her receiving of governess education), Noyeema could not develop her mental ability to discriminate between her cultural belongingness and the foreign, glittering way of life. Her situation becomes like "someone who has never seen light, hence the glow of the firefly seems to have appeared miraculous" (Rokeya, 1922, p.148). Being admitted in a hospital, Noyeema meets some Christian missionaries. As it is her first encounter with the outside world, she becomes mesmerised by their religious and cultural beliefs. With 17,000 takas in cash and massive amount of ornaments worth 25,000 takas[4], Noyeema leaves her home to join the nuns in a "mission house" (Rokeya, 1922, p.149). Noyeema receives privileged treatment from the missionaries until her money comes to an end. Finally when all her money and jewellery are spent, Noyeema ends up as a nurse in a hospital where she takes her new name "Nelly". And thus Noyeema essentially becomes homeless.

Noyeema's living a sheltered life, and her coming out of it, can be compared with Bimala's pull of the home and that of the world in Rabindranath Tagore's *Ghare Baire* (*The Home and the World*) (1916).

Bimala's fidelity to her own culture and her fascination with the Western lifestyle is represented by her love-relationships with her husband Nikhil, a product of indigenous tradition, and with her seducer Sandip, a cultural surrogate of colonised India. Noyeema has to go through awful traumas and tribulations to acquire the discrimination to see the difference between her own cultural value system and imported foreign ideals and beliefs. Likewise, Bimala also undergoes similar dreadful experiences before she realises the difference between "gold [Nikhil] and tinsel [Sandip]" (Iyengar, 1983, p.107). Both Noyeema and Bimala encounter the external world before they earn a deep and conscious rootedness in their culture. After living a secluded life in the private sphere of home or, to use Woolf's (1929) phrase, after suffering "from too rigid a restraint, too absolute a stagnation" (p.63), they suddenly found themselves face to face with a complex world, but lacked the experience and social context necessary to use this freedom effectively. Both Noyeema and Bimala suffer the same destiny of being homeless because of the lack of strong affiliation with their native cultural values.

In her essay "Dhangswer Pathey Bongiyo Mussalman" (Bengal Muslims on the Way to Decline), Rokeya gives a vivid description of how this cultural homelessness occurs in colonial context. Rokeya does not consider just going out of private life as any sign of liberty for women. Without a strong sense of belongingness and without a strong pull of one's home culture, women may not be able to achieve true independence. She draws the example of Parsi women of her time who adopted British culture without a proper appreciation of its value in their different social setting. They also used to remain in seclusion, and later on they came out of it. If this change in Parsi community happened just to imitate a foreign culture, and without proper realisation of women's liberty then, Rokeya argues, such unconscious liberty is another form of mental enslavement. For such manifestation of liberty, Rokeya (1904) is reluctant to give women any tribute because "when men wanted them to be inside seclusion they were there; now men dragged them out of it so they have come out" (p.25). Attia also touches upon this issue when she says that some women's minds "remained smothered in the *burqas* they had outwardly discarded" (*SBC* 207).

Chew and Rutherford (1993) in their *Unbecoming Daughters of the Empire* bring together personal reminiscences of some postcolonial writers who themselves suffered from cultural homelessness in their own lands. All articulate a sense of inbetweenness and their beingness in a culturally hollow space. Deshpande (1993) relates her story of cultural homelessness:

> To go to an English school, to speak English, to passionately devour books like *Alice in Wonderland* and *Treasure Island* was not, it seemed, enough to save one from being inferior. Worse – children who went to nationalist schools and shunned the touch of anything English, jeered at us who went to the 'Padre's school' as traitors. Which meant that one did not belong to that world either. Did we belong nowhere? (p.105)

Deshpande's vain childhood struggle to affiliate herself to a foreign culture, through the induction of imported colonial education, supposedly displaced and disaffiliated her from home. Her nowhereness is paradigmatic of the cultural homelessness, a common fate of her generation. Mukherjee (1993) senses the same "trauma of cultural displacement that the British system of education allegedly caused" (p.110) to render her generation, who went to elite schools, homeless. This cultural inbetweenness, which Mukherjee terms as "biculturism", creates a "daffodilized" generation who remain oblivious about their soil and about whatever they have to call theirs. Sahgal comments (1993) on "the East-West encounter" in the colonised social space, and regards the culturally displaced population, who absorbed western values, as the "brown carriers of the white culture they admired and adopted" (p.115). Sahgal recounts her personal encounter with this situatedness as well as her grappling with foreign lifestyle and her struggle to stick to home culture. Even after the independence of India, the legacy of cultural vagrancy that occurred during colonial period remains unabated. Introduction to foreign culture and oblivion to one's own belongingness generated some "mimic men", as "the experience of the Raj" robbed the displaced population of the pride in their own cultural identity (Lindblad 1993, p.125). Lindblad adds:

> We had memorized reams of English literature and learnt all about British history and the climate of the British Isles but not a word about our own country. It was virtually impossible for us to enter the vernacular school system and matriculate. (*ibid.*, p.126)

Rokeya was particularly aware of this danger of cultural dislocation when pursuing her agenda of female education. She compares a person that houses elements of different cultures with a disfigured animal (Rokeya, 1931a, p.246), who discards their beautiful local culture to embrace foreign lifestyle. She wants women to be educated on a full par with men, and at the same time does not want them to be divorced from their home culture and everything that India can feel proud of. Rokeya (1931c) states,

> When we advocated [*sic*] the education of girls we generally imply the adoption of western methods and ideals in their training to the exclusion of all that is Indian. This mistake on our part cannot be too strongly guarded against. We should not fail to set before the Indian girl the great and noble ideals of womanhood which our tradition has developed. This ideal was narrow and circumscribed in the past. We may enlarge and widen it thus increasing its excellence but what we should avoid is its total neglect and a tendency to slavish imitations of Western custom and tradition. (pp.481-482)

In her emphasis on indigenous traditions, Rokeya maintains a unique balance. While she proposes to protect her native culture, she also recommends a thorough refinement in order to protect it from the curse of unjust social customs. In her disapproval of foreign (Western) culture also, Rokeya does not suffer from any anti-West bias. She highly recommends women to selectively pick Western values without losing their own. She praises certain English "etiquette" such as "bedroom privacy" (Rokeya, 1904, p.41), which her compatriots can emulate without any qualms. Similarly, Attia is also above any anti-West bias in her effort to link Indian people to their cultural roots. When Aunt Majida tries to point towards a harsh reality of western individualism, Mrs Martin in *SBC* says, “”Majida dear, our customs are hard for you to understand. I must go back to my own people. I love you all, I love your country, but my bones must rest in my own land” (pp.48-49). The reason why Rokeya and Attia underwent a cultural shock was a slavish tendency they noticed among many of their compatriots to mimic western ethos, at the expense of irreparable ravages to their indigenous traditional values. They tried to guard especially women against this cultural vagrancy and homelessness. An attempt to reconcile superior western education and the need for attachment to one's home is common in their literary works. Western education and freedom for women must be acknowledged for the good and harm they can potentially bring to the people of India. Attia strikes a good balance through the voice of Aunt Abida, who addresses Laila, “”My child, there are certain rules of conduct that must be observed in this world without question. You have a great responsibility. You must never forget the traditions of your family no matter to what outside influences you may be exposed” (*SBC* p.28). During her conversation with Mrs Wadia and Begum Waheed, Abida proudly pronounces that “my dear niece Laila is being educated to fit into the new world, but our old traditions and culture are always kept in mind” (*ibid*., p.131). In the character of Abida, Attia also brings about a balance between two generations: one is Laila's, and the other is her aunts'. Although there remains an unbridgeable gap between Laila and her aunts, she enjoys a spiritual affinity with Abida, who “was the only one of my [Laila's] aunts whom I [Laila] had seen with a book in her hand” (*ibid*., p.139). So Abida epitomises the cultural balance that Attia espouses in her novel.

Although Abida is inculcated in education and enlightenment, she does not discard the Indian ideal of feminine self-abnegation. In her father's household, she remains “overwhelmingly conscious of her duty to her family and the family tradition” (Kaul & Jain, 2001, p.156). She dedicates herself to looking after her aged, ailing father Baba Jan. After Baba Jan's death, she was married off to an elderly man Sheikh Ejaz Ali. Even though Abida's uneven union with Ejaz has been a loveless marriage, she remains perfectly devoted to her husband. On her first visit to Abida's marital home, Laila notices that Abida "centered all attention on his [Ejaz's] care and comfort, as if everyone and everything else was secondary" (*ibid.*, p.138). Thus Attia tries to present her balanced model of Indian womanhood through the character of Abida.

Laila, Attia's spokesperson in the novel, is in a deep ambivalence. Attia depicts her heroine as a new woman who defies the harmful traditions of her society, and as someone who absorbs the western ideals of enlightenment. On the contrary, she represents Zahra as a tradition-bound girl who uncritically clings to her domestic norms. But, Laila becomes culturally dispossessed whereas Zahra has a stronger claim on cultural belongingness, as shown in Laila's statement below: "When we were small Ustaniji[5] made us recite the names of our ancestors. Zahra remembered many more than I ever did who found it difficult to name even my great-grand-father" (*ibid.*, p.39). In Indian joint family system, a distant male relative can exercise clear influence. For example, Uncle Mohsin is the son of Laila's "grandfather's father's sister's daughter"; but he is considered a "close" relative and his power and authority is felt across the family. He even rebukes Laila for her failure to "remember such close relationships" (*ibid.*, p.18). In the decision making process of Zahra's marriage, in the absence of closer male relations (as Uncle Hamid was in England at that time), Uncle Mohsin exercises his weight. Perceiving a sense of "bewilderment" among Laila and Zahra about the way he was handling Zahra's marriage, that is without Zahra's consent, he explodes in anger, "Is the girl to pass judgement on her elders? Doubt their capability to choose? Question their decision? Choose her own husband?" (*ibid.*, p.20). In an integrated joint family system in India, one's attachment with the linearity of family tree is highly valued. Laila's failure to remember her ancestors' names points towards her cultural homelessness, a supposed by-product of her induction in western education and value system.

Laila, being aware of cultural displacement, feels embarrassed in her "borrowed clothes, and with [her] false face" (*ibid.*, p.152). Attia represents feudal taluqdars as culturally a comprador class who can be termed as native carriers of a foreign culture. The un-negotiable differences between Laila and Zahra happen for two obvious reasons: they are colonials and they receive governess education. Both these factors render them culturally divided. In the end of *SBC*, Laila recounts her cultural split-up with Zahra and the family integration in the following way: "In the end, inevitably, we quarrelled, and though we made up before we parted I realised that the ties which had kept families together for centuries had been loosened beyond repair" (p.303). The physical disintegration of the family and of the country was sparked off by a subtler breakdown in the cultural fabric of the home.

Works Cited:

Anand, M. R. (1978). Profile of Attia Hosain. *Commonwealth Quarterly* (New Delhi), 3(9), 1-12.

Butalia, U. (1998). *The Other Side of Silence: Voices from the Partition of India*. India: Penguin Books.

Chew, S. & Rutherford, A. (Ed.) (1993). *Unbecoming Daughters of the Empire*. UK: Dangaroo Press 1993

Deshpande, S. (1993). Them and Us. In S. Chew, & A. Rutherford (Ed.). *Unbecoming Daughters of the Empire* (pp. 101-106). UK: Dangaroo Press.

George, R. M. (1996). *The Politics of Home: Postcolonial Relocations and Twentieth-Century Fiction*. UK: Cambridge University Press.

Gilbert, S. M., & Gubar, S. (2000). *The Madwoman in the Attic: The Woman Writer And The Nineteenth-Century Literary Imagination* (2nd ed.). London; New Haven: Yale University Press.

Gomis, A. (2002). Purdah and Power: Unveiling the Links. *Revista Canaria de Estudios Ingleses*, 45, 101-119.

Hosain, A. (1992). *Sunlight on a Broken Column* (1961). Delhi: Penguin Books

Hosain, A. (1988). *Phoenix Fled* (1953). London: Virago.

Iyengar, K. R. S. (1983). *Indian Writings in English* (3rd ed.). Delhi: Sterling Publishers.

Kaul, R. K., & Jain, J. (2001). *Attia Hosain: A Diptych Volume*. India: Rawat Publications.

Kidwai, A. R. (2005). "Death of a beautiful woman": Qurratul Ayn Hyder on Attia Hosain. *Journal of the Faculty of Arts* (Aligarh Muslim University), 3:1-2, 59-66.

Lindblad, I. (1993). The Irresistible Anglo-Filiation of Ishrat. In S. Chew, & A. Rutherford (Ed.). *Unbecoming Daughters of the Empire* (pp.121-128). UK: Dangaroo Press.

Martin, B. & Mohanty, C. T. (1988). Feminist Politics: What's Home Got to Do with It?. In B. Martin, & C. T. Mohanty, *Feminist Studies/ Critical Studies* (pp.191-212). UK: Macmillan.

Mukherjee, M. (1971). *The Twice Born Fiction: Themes and Techniques of the Indian Novel in English.* New Delhi: Heinemann.

Mukherjee, M. (1993). Growing up by the Ganga. In S. Chew, & A. Rutherford (Ed.). *Unbecoming Daughters of the Empire* (pp. 107-112). UK: Dangaroo Press.

Nabar, V. (2000). Fragmenting nations and lives: *Sunlight on a Broken Column*. In H. Trivedi, & R. Allen (Ed.). *Literature and Nation: Britain and India, 1800 to 1900* (pp.121-137). London: Routledge.

Rokeya, B. (1904). *Motichur-I.* In A. Qadir (Ed.), *Rokeya Rachanabali* (2nd ed.) (1999) (pp. 1-54). Dhaka: Bangla Academy.

Rokeya, B. (1905). *Sultana's Dream*. In A. Qadir (Ed.), *Rokeya Rachanabali* (2nd ed.) (1999) (pp. 461-474). Dhaka: Bangla Academy.

Rokeya, B. (1913, September 30). Letter to Mohd. Yasin. In A. Qadir (Ed.), *Rokeya Rachanabali* (2nd ed.) (1999) (p. 504). Dhaka: Bangla Academy.

Rokeya, B. (1922). *Motichur-I*. In A. Qadir (Ed.), *Rokeya Rachanabali* (2nd ed.) (1999) (pp. 55-182). Dhaka: Bangla Academy.

Rokeya, B. (1931a). Dhongser Pathe Bongio Mussalman. In A. Qadir (Ed.), *Rokeya Rachanabali* (2nd ed.) (1999) (pp. 244-247). Dhaka: Bangla Academy.

Rokeya, B. (1931b). *Aborodhbasini*. In A. Qadir (Ed.), *Rokeya Rachanabali* (2nd ed.) (1999) (pp. 371-405). Dhaka: Bangla Academy.

Rokeya, B. (1931c). Education Ideals for the Modern Indian Girl. In A. Qadir (Ed.), *Rokeya Rachanabali* (2nd ed.) (1999) (pp. 478-483). Dhaka: Bangla Academy.

Sahgal, N (1993). The Schizophrenic Imagination. In S. Chew, & A. Rutherford (Ed.). *Unbecoming Daughters of the Empire* (pp. 113-120). UK: Dangaroo Press.

Said. E. (1991). Patriotism. *The Nation* (July 15/22, 1991), 253(3), 116.

Said, E. (1986). *After the Last Sky*. USA: Columbia University Press.

Shamsie, M. (2004). Attia Hosain (1913-1998). *The Literary Encyclopedia*. Retrieved September 29, 2004 from http://www.litencyc.com/php/speople.php?rec=true&UID=2216

Tagore, R. (1919). *The Home and the World* (*Ghare Baire* [1916], trans. S. Tagore). London: Macmillan.

Woolf , V. (1927). *To the Lighthouse* (1964). UK: Penguin Books.

Woolf, V. (1929). *A Room of One's Own* (1993). In M. Barrett (Ed.), *A Room of One's Own/Three Guineas* (pp.1-116). London: Penguin Books.

Woolf, V. (1938). *Three Guineas* (1993). In M. Barrett (Ed.), *A Room of One's Own/Three Guineas* (pp.117-272). London: Penguin Books.

Notes and References

1. Woolf (1938) touches upon this alien status of a woman in her homeland when she says in *Three Guineas* that "by law she becomes a foreigner if she marries a foreigner" (p.233).

2. The word *harem* in its original sense connotes sacredness, as the Muslim holy place in Makkah is called Masjidul Harem (the Sacred Mosque). But down the ages, it was corrupted and became associated with the secluded domestic space, to which wives and concubines were relegated.

3. The plot of the novel covers also most of 1930s, which Srinivas Iyengar (1983) calls "a packed decade" with many political events of modern independent India, such as: "the Gandhian salt satyagraha movements of 1930 and 1932, the three Round Table Conferences, the passing of the Government of India Act of 1935, the introduction of Provincial Autonomy in 1937, the Gandhian movements for Harijan uplift and Basic Education, the organization of Marxist parties of diverse hues (the Congress Socialists, the Royalists, the Communists), the involvement in the War in 1939, the schism in the Congress leading to the expulsion of Subhas Chandra Bose and his eventual escape to Germany and Japan" (p.332).

4. Such figures in Rokeya's time were big amounts of money.

5. Female family teacher; an Indian counterpart of English governess.

Chapter - 5

Feminism and Feminist Utopia in Rokeya Sakhawat Hossain's *Sultana's Dream*

Seemin Hasan

'Woman' is a crucial feminist term. Concepts of femininity and how to conceptualize the feminist subject have been the focus of scholars like Simone de Beauvoir, Kate Miller and Julia Kristeva. Others, like Chandra Mohanty, have identified race, location and ethnicity as their central viewpoint.[1] Western feminist discourse has traditionally been very patronizing to the third world woman. The typical third world woman has been defined as family oriented, domestic, religious, semi-literate and indecisive. The third world 'other' is contrasted with the white woman who is depicted as sexually liberated, educated, secular and always in control of her life. This attitude has its roots in the western belief that the third world woman has not 'evolved' as much as her white counterpart and will be able to do so only when she adopts Western definitions and specifications. In such contexts, the significance of the local gender relations and cultural specifications is ignored altogether. Rokeya Sakhawat Hossain's short story, 'Sultana's Dream', when read in this perspective, reveals that Western perceptions are not always universally applicable. Even early literary works by third world women, when judged in their own historical, political and ethnic contexts, prove that the third world woman was not always a powerless victim of the patriarchy but was educated, aware and secular in her own way.

Rokeya Sakhawat Hossain is one of the earliest women writers of the Indian subcontinent who sought self-development and also attempted to critique the inequalities of the social conditions. She is grouped with other women writers, also of Bengali origin, like Khairunnisa Khatun, Girindramohini and Krishnabhabhini. While Rokeya Hossain also wrote in English, the others wrote mostly in Bengali. All these women writers, in their works, redefine the goal of education for their intellectual freedom; question the relevance of tradition, of woman worship, answer male allegations of Westernization, justify their dress sense on the basis of propriety, prescribe economic freedom for women and justify even their sexual freedom. Infact, they provide a pre-history to the later developments of feminism[2].

Rokeya Hossain was born in 1880 at Pairaband, Rangpur district, which is now part of Bangladesh. Her father was an aristocratic landowner who had unflinching faith in conservative values. Like most Muslim girls of her generation, Rokeya grew up in strict *purdah* and was privately tutored in Arabic and Urdu. An elder brother, Ibrahim Sabir, taught her English. Later she dedicated her Bengali work *Padmarag* to him. She dedicated *Sultana's Dream* to her sister, Karimunnisa. At the age of sixteen, she was married to Khan Bahadur Syed Sakhawat Hussain, twenty-four years her senior.

Bengal was the first province in India to encounter Western modernity as Calcutta, until 1911, was the imperial capital. The colonial government's critique of Indian society and particularly the position of women generated a crisis among the educated classes. In the course of the nineteenth century they initiated reforms to uplift the condition of women and also envisioned new roles for them. The Bengali intelligentsia felt that a respectable identity could be created through the way the new, reformed, educated class positioned its women within its social sphere. Thus, at the time Rokeya Sakhawat Hussain came of age, a 'new woman' was defined by the Indian patriarchy. The 'new woman' fulfilled roles as perfect wife, mother, manager of household and also of a restricted social life. Her status, in her own household, inspite of being responsible for its smooth functioning, was higher only than that of minor children and servants. The true gentlewoman, as defined by the patriarchy, at this time, was pure, unsullied, sacrificing and selfless.

Normative texts in the form of domestic manuals, on the lines of British domestic manuals filled the urban market[3]. These texts were secular and were considered appropriate for any married woman irrespective of religion and caste. Thus, the discourse on women and family was highly polarized along gender and class lines. The so-called 'new woman' remained subjected to a highly stratified patriarchy and was accorded little or no power. Partha Chatterjee claims that Indian nationalism thus resolved the women's question by locating it within an inner domain[4].

After marriage Rokeya moved to Bhagalpur, Bihar, where her husband was serving as a magistrate. Here she came in contact with formally educated elitist women and in their company perfected her English. Her husband encouraged her to write and to pursue reformist and philanthropic activities.

Sultana's Dream was published in 1905 in the *Indian Ladies Magazine* published from Madras and co-edited by Sarojini Naidu. Women's writing in English, at this time, was relegated to women's magazines and dismissed as whims of the over-protected, upper-class, English-speaking women, uttered as a diversion. Infact, the pre-independence women writers were charged with constructing an imaginary community. The disciplinary gatekeepers kept at bay those dimensions of cultural history, cultural economy and canon building that affected women. For a long time women's literature remained a marginalized area of critical study. Historically, low value has always been set on the words and experiences of women.

Initial reaction to Rokeya's writings was hostile. She was charged with embarrassing the conservative Muslim society. Some accused her of supporting the Christian Tract Society that had been issuing critical pamphlets on Islam. Others treated her departure from patriarchal norms as a departure from morality and branded her a fallen woman. Abid Hussain wrote in the Bengali magazine *Sadhana* in 1921, that the seclusion of men in Ladyland in *Sultana's Dream* was:

> ...a reaction of the prevailing oppression and vulnerability of our women...perhaps Mrs. R.S. Hossain wrote this to create a sense of self-confidence among the very vulnerable Bengali women... that women may possess faculties and

> talents equivalent to or greater than men-that they are capable of developing themselves to a stage where they may attain complete mastery over nature without any help from men and create a new world of perfect beauty, great wealth and goodness-this is what 'Sultana's Dream' depicts…I hope the male readers of 'Sultana's dream' would try to motivate the women of their families towards self-realization[5].

Sultana's Dream is a feminist utopia that cuts across time and space and explores the feminine inner self. Marginalized and also part of a minority, women often turn to fantasy as a literary mode of destroying a hostile society and replacing it with a new, congenial one. The author, thus, becomes the epitome of subversion, the destroyer of social, political and economic barriers. She, too, acquires a new identity. Friedman comments:

> Women experimentalists declare themselves on the side of the ruptured and unreliable narrative, for in spaces created by ruptures and anxiety, provoked by the unreliable, they continue the project of a feminine discourse that not only can bear narrative, but can provide a hopeful alternative[6].

Rokeya Sakhawat Hossain's work antedates many Western feminist utopias with similar themes. The nineteenth and twentieth centuries have witnessed a variety of feminist envisioning of utopia. Mary Shelley's *The Last Man* published in 1826, deals with the efforts of Lionel Verney to establish a utopia on earth. The central character is male but is patterned on the author. Women are largely subservient. For most utopias written in this period by women, the issues were religious and educational. Mary Griffith's *Three Hundred Years Hence* focuses on peace and prosperity. Feminist utopias which, like Rokeya Hossain's story, deal with sex- role reversal include Annie Denton Cridge's *Man's Rights or How Would You Like It?* E.M. Broner's *A Weave of Women*, Margaret Atwood's 'The Handmaid's Tale' and Sally Miller Gearhart's *The Wanderground*[7].

Like most feminist utopias *Sultana's Dream* is a direct exploration of gender-pivotal society. The basic premise is that a group of women create a nearly all female society.

Dream sequences, shadowy and associative memory, futuristic visions are interwoven in Rokeya's story. The dream mode is used as a powerful tool to expand the boundaries of human thought. Sultana, the protagonist, dreams of an ideal world, Ladyland, where the lost matriarchal society is regained. The word 'Sultana' refers to the wife of the 'Sultan' or the ruler. The name of the protagonist serves as an ironic contrast to the scientist Queen of Ladyland who is independent of any male support. Ladyland is a utopian space since it represents an ideal feminist space. *Sultana's Dream* employs utopia to inspire those women who suffer within patriarchal societies. Ladyland represents the liberating prospects of women, particularly Rokeya herself.

The story can be seen as representing a satirical utopian society as the power of males is taken away and given to females. It is a contrast to the society of Rokeya's times and to the idea of separated space, which occurred within society. The patriarchal order is inverted and Sultana is amazed to find the men confined to a *mardana* designed on the lines of a *zenana* or the inner sections of a conventional Muslim household where the women lived and the men were not permitted to enter. 'They should not do anything, excuse me; they are fit for nothing. Only catch them and put them into the *zenana*'.[8] (SD p.6) Sultana is told. The men lost their position because they believed in muscle power and warfare rather than intellectual power. When invaded by a neighbouring kingdom, they exhausted themselves completely and proved themselves incapable of defeating the enemy. Sultana's escort informs her:

> On the following day, the Queen called upon all the men to retire into zenanas for the sake of honour and liberty. Wounded and tired as they were, they took the order for a boon! They bowed low and entered the zenanas without uttering a single word of protest (SD p.10).

The men continue to stay in the *mardanas* and attend to domestic chores. Sultana is surprised because she believed that the confinement to *zenana* was women's unquestioned destiny. The iconoclastic discovery that women could be free fills her with excitement. Sultana also believed that men had sharper brains than women. She is told that:

> Women's brains are somewhat quicker than men's. Ten years ago, when the military officers called our scientific discoveries 'a sentimental nightmare' some of the young ladies wanted to say something in reply to these remarks. But both Lady principals restrained them and said, they should reply, not by word, but deed, if ever they got the opportunity. And they had not long to wait for that opportunity. (SD p.9)

Sultana now develops a new ability to escape the limitations imposed by the patriarchy. Rokeya's story provides the leverage for displacing the system of concepts or procedures of patriarchy. Rokeya herself observed *purdah*. She viewed *purdah* as a restrictive device that kept women submissive and prevented them from expressing themselves. She thought that if men could not control themselves enough to not accost women, they were the ones who ought to be locked in *purdah* and in the *mardana* as it was called in Ladyland. Rokeya's own observation of *purdah* lends her character the credibility to discuss the issue. In the context, the story serves as a call to awareness of females under patriarchal oppression. The readers, thus, consider the story much more than a mere fantasy. It appears as a treatise about injustice to women in *purdah* written ironically.

Ladyland is full of flourishing, ornamental gardens, is free from pollution and disease and is a place where nobody ever dies young. Women, under the leadership of a scientist Queen look after the political, commercial and educational affairs. Ladyland is a utopia where science, technology and humanism work in unison to make women self-reliant. Women emerge as positive entities rather than as domineering and powerful matriarchs. The acknowledged legislators of the patriarchy viz. tradition and custom fade into the background. Patriarchal oppressions become meaningless in this utopia. Sultana's escort comments, 'A lion is stronger then a man, but it does not enable him to dominate the human race.' (SD p.5)

Education is the basis of these women's achievements. The theme of education is central to *Sultana's Dream* Gender bias, in Rokeya's lifetime had resulted in limited access and lowered prioritization of academia for women. Sultana is informed that a number of universities have been established by the Queen. Active research programmes have resulted in a number of very practical inventions like the storm-stopping machine. This consists of a balloon attached to pipes. Water is drawn from the atmosphere through the pipe to stop cloud formation. A second invention is the creation of flying cars. The flying cars are structures in the conventional shape with hydrogen balls of different weights attached to the frames. On the other car are electricity driven wing blades that propel the car in the air. Other inventions include artificial fountains and solar—heat machines in which heat is concentrated and stored.

A distinction is made between 'feminine' and 'masculine' technology. Feminine technology is based on solar energy, is environment-friendly and non-lethal. 'Masculine' technology includes weapons, is industrial, chemical and lethal and therefore unnatural and unfriendly to the environment. The dichotomy between genders in this text draws attention not only to the suppression of females but also to what may be lost by not considering their input as issues of great importance.

Sultana departs from Ladyland using the dream mode once again. She carries home the realization that women of Ladyland have an irrepressible zest for life. They believe in self-reliance and a universalistic concept of shared humanity that does not admit any discrimination on the basis of either caste, creed or gender. In *Sultana's Dream*, apart from the fight for equal opportunities and education for women, the intention of the author is also to portray women as equal if not superior to men in many ways.

Rokeya's utopian feminist fiction presents visions of what a society would be like without gender structures and inegalitarian gender relationships. She treats the patriarchal reality as a threatening space for women whereas her utopian story provides the liberating space.

Notes and References

1. Chandra Mohanty, 'Under Western Eyes: Feminist Scholarship and Colonial Discourses'; *Feminist Review*, no. 30, Autumn 1988.
2. For details of these women writers see Malini Bhattacharya and Abhijit Sen's *Talking of Power: Early Writings of Bengali Women From the Mid-Nineteenth Century to Beginning of the Twentieth Century* (Calcutta: Stree,2004)
3. Some of the Bengali manuals were Maulana Ashraf Ali's *Bihishti Zewar* and Uma Debi's *Balika Jivana*. Some of the British manuals were G.Oram's The *Book of Domestic Duties* and Emma Drake's *What a Young Wife Ought to Know.*
4. Partha Chatterjee 'Nationalist Resolution of the Women's Question', in K.Sangari & Sudesh Vaid's (eds.) *Recasting Women* (New Brunwick; Rutgers UP, 1990) pp. 233-253.
5. R. Mohan 'Begum Rokeya Sakhawat Hossain (1880-1932)'. http://www.haverford.edu/engl/engl277b/contexts/rokeya_hosain.html.
6. G. Ellen Friedman and Miriam Fuchs's' Contexts and Continuities: An Introduction to Women's Experimental Fiction in English", *Breaking the Sequence* (Princeton: PUP,1989), p27.
7. For detailed lists of feminist utopias bibliographies and reviews consult the following website: http:// www. Feministsf.org/femsf
8. Rokeya Sakhawat Hossain *Sultana's Dream and Padmarag – The Feminist Utopias* (New Delhi: Penguin Books, 2005). All subsequent quotations from 'Sultana's Dream' are from this edition.

Chapter - 6

Suffering of Women and the Question of Plural Identity: Amitava Kumar's Reading of the Politics of Faith in *Husband of a Fanatic*

Mohd. Asim Siddiqui

Writing about Amitava Kumar's *Bombay- London- New York* (2002), Pankaj Mishra, the author of *The Romantics: A Novel*, commented on the element of tenderness in Kumar's writing and praised him for 'illuminating the individual and collective histories that a young literature emerges from'.1 Kumar's *Husband of a Fanatic* (2004), a work marked by his tender feelings and sincere approach, also takes up the painful histories of a number of people and the collective predicament of a community. The form of the book defies an easy classification as it is poised somewhere between a travelogue, an expose, a collection of personal essays and a sort of non-fictional Bildungsroman. The 'characters' in the book are people existing in real life, people whom Kumar meets in his journey to places as varied as London, Ahmedabad, Patna, Bombay, Delhi, Srinagar and Karachi. But the meeting with the people—a number of them are Muslim women—also is an attempt on the part of Kumar to understand the suffering of the ordinary people, most importantly the suffering of Muslim men and women in independent India. It also is an attempt on his part to discover his identity—whether it is Hindu or plural—and to understand the forces which are hell bent on hoisting on him, or for that matter on others, an identity of their naming. In the title of the book the word fanatic ironically refers to Amitava Kumar's Muslim wife. The irony lies in the fact that following the rise to power of the radical right-wing element in Indian politics and the changing international scenario—end of cold war, 'clash-of-civilization' thesis, 9/11, India's relations with Pakistan—the word fanatic is synonymous with the word Muslim. Kumar tries to learn first hand "how

Muslims felt in India (especially)...during a riot."[2] Using a storyteller's skill and a novelist's sense of organization Kumar weaves together a critique on the politics of faith in independent India in an international context. The probe into the politics of faith and Nationalism necessitates a discussion of Partition, Kashmir, demolition of Babri Masjid, the reality of communal riots, the Gujarat mayhem and the effect of 9/11 on Muslims. Kumar never fights shy of treating these issues with sincerity and honesty.

At one place in the book Kumar quotes Albert Camus who said that 'By definition the writer cannot serve those who make history: he serves those who have to live it. (p.276)' Camus's opinion is obviously flawed as one can mention any number of writers in our time, particularly brown sahibs from VS Naipaul, Salman Rushdie in fiction to Irshad Manji and many others in non-fiction who are out to prove themselves to be more faithful than the king. Then there are those writers who are or were in the grip of the established ideology without their being conscious of its sinister hold. But Camus's construction is true about Arundhati Roy who is not tempted by huge advances, who donates her prize money to organizations fighting fascism and who boldly takes up the cause of impoverished people affected by the wrong policies of the government. It is also true of Amitava Kumar's sympathetic reporting of the suffering of the people particularly women who suffered badly in Gujarat and who continue to suffer in different camps in inhuman conditions.

The book opens with the description of Shama, a Muslim political activist, who is carrying out relief work in different camps in Ahmedabad following Gujarat violence. An outraged Shama takes Amitava Kumar to meet a number of girls and women –Ruksana's and Razia's suffering is specially mentioned— who were raped, their men folk brutally killed and they forced to live in the relief camps. It is really ironic that there were also weddings in the camps but the reason for these weddings in places as inappropriate as relief camps was Muslims' anxiety and a strong sense of insecurity particularly about the future of their girls. Amitava Kumar makes it obvious what has been pointed out by quite a few commentators that rape was used as a weapon in Gujarat carnage The commonly heard expression 'crime against women' appears in all its naked colour in this land of Gandhi during this period. The result of a meticulously planned brutality inflicted on a sizable population may fill a person with a sense of insecurity but Amitava Kumar knows that because of his Hindu identity he can walk freely into the offices of VHP and other extremist Hindu organizations. He realizes that even theoretically he could not have been one of the victims of this carnage. He is appalled to see prejudice against Muslims in all walks of life .During his visit to a school in the Muslim area of Juhapura in Ahmedabad he is particularly moved by the appeal of Reshma, a fourteen year old school girl, who cannot understand why her area was called 'mini-Pakistan'. 'We are also Indians….We are not foreigners. We should have rights as Indian citizens (p.123).' Amitava Kumar knows that the problem was that her teachers themselves were not fair and were heavily prejudiced against her community.

As if to show the brutality of the Gujarat mayhem and the humanity of its victims, Kumar mentions the suffering of Noorjahan, a woman gang-raped during the riots. However, what pains Noorjahan now the most is her realization that she lost her pets in the Gujrat tragedy. Her cats as well as other pets, which included a parrot named Raja, were killed by the mob. 'Those animals loved me. More than human beings, I loved the animals and the birds. There is love between animals (p.34).' The German philosopher Kant was of the view that 'we can judge the heart of a man by his treatment of animals.'[3] The ugly incident reveals not only the character of Noorjahan but also that of the people who went on a killing spree.

Amitava Kumar's treatment of the communal politics also takes him back to Bhagalpur riots which rocked Bihar in the 80s and took a heavy toll of Muslims' lives. Though many lives were lost and many families ruined in these riots, his special mention of Rasheeda's problem is also his tribute to this brave woman. Rasheeda bore very stoically the loss of her, husband, the sole breadwinner in the family, and refused to live on others' pity. Amitava Kumar knows that despite Rasheeda's successful effort in educating her daughters—they were all science graduates—their degrees may not procure jobs for them. It is not only a pointer to the dismal employment scenario in Bihar but also to the prevalence of prejudice against Muslims. He is also touched by Rasheeda's anxiety about the marital future of her daughters. This again suggests that a girl's good education notwithstanding, the worry uppermost in the minds of the parents is the marriage of their daughter(s). However, despite Rasheeda maintaining a brave face the scars of her tragedy would not heal easily. She would always see in her dreams the necks of her children and how she 'would try to bend down and pick up my kids in my arms (p.288).'

The life of the people affected by the violence in Kashmir Valley is also taken up by Amitava Kumar in this book. A horrible and frightening reality of Kashmir is the gradually increasing number of people who have simply disappeared after being arrested by the security forces; there are about 3000 of these young men. There is no information with any one about their being dead or alive. Pårveena runs from pillar to post to have any information about her son Javed who was taken away by the security forces. Ironically the security forces were looking for a militant whose name was Javed. Parveena , like Rasheeda, is a brave and affectionate woman and is a source of hope for many people. She is the chairperson of the Association of the Parents of Disappeared Persons. One woman , mentioned by Amitava Kumar, who banks upon Parveena for help is Shafiqa whose husband disappeared, turning her into a 'half widow'. The individual histories of these two women are symptomatic of life in Kashmir. There is now a growing number of mental cases in hospitals though Sadqat Rahman, the lady doctor looking after the psychiatry ward, links this phenomenon to a general increase in the number of mental illnesses all over the world.

Amitava Kumar illuminates not only the personal histories of others' life; he turns to his life too to arrive at the understanding of some issues which trouble him. At one level all writings are autobiographical. This book also is an autobiography though it does not describe every thing about the writer's life. Hanif Kureishi points out that 'most of the significant moments of one's life are insignificant to other people. It is showing how and why they are significant and also why they may seem absurd, that is art.'[4] It is debatable if Kumar is interested in the issue of art here, but his inter-religious marriage, certainly a significant moment in his life, compels the writer in him to explore issues of identity, Hindu-Muslim relations, particularly the problems of couples into inter-religious marriages at socio-political level, and the politics of faith in independent India. In keeping with the form of the book, Kumar illuminates the individual cases of inter-religious marriages often not confining himself to just the real people into these marriages but also taking up the portrayal of some such marriages in films and literature. He mentions the failed love affair of Lata and Kabir Durrani in Vikram Seth's *A Suitable Boy*. Despite Lata's love for this Muslim boy and despite her mother being not more prejudiced against Muslims than most upper-caste Hindu women of her time and background, the affair cannot culminate into marriage. In recent times, to mention a different case, *Gadar*, a popular Hindi film set in Amritsar and Lahore against the background of Partition, shows a Muslim girl from an aristocratic family marrying a Sikh. The girl, left behind at the railway station in a melee, was saved by the Sikh in question. *Gadar's* plot reminded Kumar of Urvashi Butalia's book on Partition titled *The Other Side of Silence* which narrates the story of one Zainab who was sold to a Jat peasant after being abducted from a refugee party bound for Pakistan. Amitava Kumar relates these examples to the real life situation of Nazrana Khatoon, a girl living in a remand home in Patna. The remand home housed quite a few women who had married outside their religion. Nazrana Khatoon, originally belonging to a small town in Bihar, had married a Hindu and had converted to Hinduism and had christened herself Munni Devi. She was in the remand home because her husband was behind bars on the false charges of abduction and rape. Amitava Kumar finds her emotional reaction to the movie, set during the period of Partition remarkable as 'the story enacted across the border of India and Pakistan had found form and significance far away inside a small country-town in eastern India (pp.44-45).'

Drawing on the works of feminist scholars like Butalia, Ritu Menon and Kamla Bhasin and the testimony of social workers like Mridula Sarabhai and Krishna Thapar, Kumar discusses the forgotten stories of women affected by the riots during Partition. 'The women who were abducted have been lost to history, their stories drowned in silence; and those women who have been killed by their own families have become symbols of sacrifice and their deaths turned into tales of martyrdom (p.224).' The fate of many women on both sides of the border who were forced to convert and marry is too well known. The issue compelled the governments of the two countries to come out with a joint declaration to the effect that forced conversion would not be recognized and that 'the women and girls who have been abducted must be restored to their families, and every effort must be made by the Governments and their officers concerned to trace and recover such women and girls (p.225).' What was particularly regrettable about this gesture was the fact that women were treated as disposable and dispensable commodities who had no say and choice in the matter. Many women did not want to return to their original families. On this issue the attitudes of Muslims differed from those of Hindus. Amitava Kumar quotes the words of Kamlaben Patel who worked in the relief camps for women:

> A Hindu woman felt that she had been made impure, had become sullied, was no longer a *pativrata*. A Muslim woman did not feel like this. It was not in her blood, it is in our blood. We feel we have been polluted, we are no longer worthy of showing our faces in public. How can we face our families now when we go back? We would reassure the woman saying, 'See how many times your father has come to fetch you.' Even then they would feel ashamed of themselves because this tradition is so deeply ingrained in us. And Muslim women were not stigmatized by society (p.227).

Kamlaben Patel's words are couched in the vocabulary of 'us' and 'they' and appear to view the thing from a Hindu angle. Though it does not seem very plausible that Muslim women were not stigmatized by abduction and rape, the Muslim society was probably more tolerant towards taking its women back than the Hindu society.

Amitava Kumar is certainly not amused to learn that his entirely personal decision to marry Mona, Asma Jahangir's niece, was viewed by Hindu nationalists like Jagdish Barotia and Professor Dalmia, Kumar considers them bigots, in terms of power and dominance. Drawing his vocabulary from an aggressively patriarchal and obscurantist reading of Hinduism fed on the hatred of Muslims Mr Barotia, though unhappy with Kumar for his secular views, does not mind too much his marrying a Muslim girl. What is unpardonable in his opinion is the marriage of a Muslim boy with a Hindu girl; to him it was the conspiracy of Muslims to defile Hindu girls as (he explains) can bee seen in the marriage of many film stars.' It is for this reason that Geeta Behn, a devout Hindu married to a Muslim man, is killed by a Hindu mob. This intolerance is also responsible for the killing of Rupu Khan, a young man from Bhagalpur who did the impermissible by falling in love with a Hindu girl and eloping with her. In his effort to meet couples into inter-religious marriages, Amitava Kumar has no difficulty in meeting Sagar Rao who is married to a Muslim woman. In fact, Sagar Rao's life is not affected by events in Gujarat as his Hindu identity not only is a shield for him but also for his Muslim wife. No such advantage is enjoyed by Aziz who is married to a Hindu woman and unlike Sagar Rao has to hide his identity and has to live constantly in a state of panic.

Kumar's own marriage had its share of problems His problem is made worse by the fact that he did not only marry a Muslim, he married a Pakistani Muslim girl, that too in Pakistan during the Kargil War. It is true that neither Mona nor her family is shown to be very conservative by Amitava Kumar. However, as is the case in India, Mona's mother, feeling the pressure of living in a conservative Pakistani society, insists that Kumar takes a Muslim name though the word conversion is not mentioned even once by Mona's family. Kumar can marry Mona but only when he becomes Safdar Ali. Kumar's mother, though possibly more accepting of religious differences, is justifiably hurt at Kumar's 'conversion'. Much as Kumar would have liked to announce his plural identity, partaking of both the Hindu and Muslim influences, he cannot do it without offending a significant number of people including his family. The traditional set-up in India and Pakistan would not allow anyone to have a multiple religious identity. One's religious identity is fixed; in fact, it overrides all other identities in times of communal trouble. It is a different thing that at a philosophical level Intizar

Husain, the famous Urdu writer who migrated from India to Pakistan, can declare himself to be both Muslim and Hindu. But the day to day life in India makes it difficult for any one to live with a plural identity. Amitava Kumar's search for and identification with a plural identity pits him against V.S. Naipaul's idea of 'purity and fixity in religion (p.207)' He repeatedly makes the point that 'communities have grown historically in dialogue with each other. Their influences are mixed and shared. They have long-standing histories in the places where they have flourished. If you go far back in time, surely all of us are converts (p.207).'

Notes and References

1. Pankaj Mishra, New Catalog, http://www.thenewpress.com/books/husband.htm

2. Amitava Kumar, *Husband of a Fanatic* (New Delhi: Penguin Books), p.214.All further references to this book are indicated in the text of the paper by page numbers only.

3. Quoted by Justine Hankins, 'Our Character Reflected in Our Pets', *The Hindu* (Delhi) September 6, 2005.p.11.

4. Hanif Kureishi, 'Something Given: Reflections on Writing', http://www.hanifkureishi.com/something_given.html

Chapter - 7

Representation of Muslim Women in Qurratulain Hyder's *Agle Janam Mohe Bitia Na Kijo* and Ruskin Bond's *A Flight of Pigeons*: A Comparative study

Sami Rafiq

Qurratulain Hyder's "Agle Janam Mohe Bitia Na Kijo" (Don't Make Me a Daughter in the Next Birth) and Ruskin Bond's *A Flight of Pigeons* centre around the world of Muslim women. Even though they are set in different time periods of Indian history there is a strong thread of similarity that runs through these two works. A comparative analysis of the representation of Muslim women in these two texts reveals not only the suppression of women in male dominated households but also instances of close personal relationships between women cutting across different barriers, a female vision of reality and the hidden strengths of women.

Hyder's story shows the struggle of two impoverished orphaned sisters, Rushke Qamar and Jamilan (who is crippled in the legs) towards reclaiming their identity in a male dominated world. Bond's story, set in Shahjahanpur against the background of the revolt of 1857, is about the survivors of an Englishman's family (after he was killed by the rebels). The novella discusses the contact of the Englishman's family with a Muslim household where they take refuge till the rebels are overcome by the British.

Both stories present a picture of a patriarchal set up where women are enclosed in the four walls of the house and have to lead lives of compliance and obedience to men folk. They are mere objects and playthings in the hands of men. Men, on the other hand, may do what they like with their lives, are free to marry as many times as they wish to and have the freedom to seek the fulfillment of their wishes. In *A Flight of*

Pigeons the Labadoor family (that consisted of Ruth, her mother, grandmother, sister and servants) takes refuge in the house of Lala Ramjimal. But after sometime they are forcibly taken away by the rebel Javed (a *pathan*) who had taken a fancy to Ruth. He is intent on marrying Ruth even though he is already married. Javed's infatuation with Ruth can yield different kinds of readings. His colonial self is attracted towards somebody who otherwise is considered unattainable. At another level the rebel in him wants to exercise some power over his rulers. The institution of marriage has taken a lot of beating from feminists for giving undue power to man and no wonder Javed tries to use this weapon to 'control' his rulers. It is interesting to note that in some feminist circles there is a talk of phallic imperialism which converts women into "metaphorical blacks". In the special context of the story Ruth, because of being a woman, is the metaphorical black and hence liable to be colonized while Javed, because of being a man, is the metaphorical 'white' master. Javed's relationship with his wife Khan Begum, on the other hand, is to be understood in the context of the traditional husband-wife relationship in patriarchy. The following lines express not only the nature of this oppressive relationship but are also suggestive of a Muslim woman's place in a patriarchal set-up.

"The greater fool you, Javed, for depriving the child of her father, and breaking the flower from its stem before it had bloomed!" said Khan Begum 'What did you say, Qabil?' he asked sharply. "No, don't repeat it again. The demon is only slumbering in my breast, and it will take little to rouse it."[1]

She is using poetic images to convey to Javed that he is a cruel male plunderer who had snatched a flower before it has bloomed. In other words, he has forced, through his passion or lust, to turn a young girl into a woman before her time. It shows that Khan Begum has been used to seeing this sort of thing in her household where girls are forced to be women before they are ready.

In Hyder's story, the Deputy expresses his desire to his wife that he wishes to marry Rushke Qamar who is one of the many refugees who pay rent for lodging in the basement of his house Furqan Manzil:

The Deputy's wife was holding the mirror before him. Deputy Sahib was humming and busy beautifying himself. Suddenly he said – "Biwi— should I propose (temporary marriage) to Rashke Qamar? The Deputy's wife put the mirror on the stool and…dragging her flat heeled shoes went towards her room,"[2]

The language of the Deputy's wife is that of silence. It is a silent rage that vents itself on Rushke Qamar and her family, turning them out of the lodgings. The silence is emblematic of Muslim women enclosed within the four walls of the house and bearing the injustices meted out to them without uttering a murmur. But it is a silence that is potentially powerful and can turn into vengeance. It makes the wife scheme to get rid of the other woman without arousing the ire of her husband. The case is similar in Bond's story: Javed silences his wife with a threat, but she manages to get the support of the other women of the household who prevent Javed from marrying Ruth.

Justifiably Robin Lakoff's reading of feminist texts convinces him that 'the marginality and powerlessness of women is reflected in…the ways women are expected to speak.'[3]

The very fact that Rushke Qamar and Jamilan are lured by Agha Farhad who promises them fame as radio singers, throws light on how, forced by poverty, these women are powerless to fight their exploitation. They are introduced to Verma Sahib who runs The Song Birds Club and who has a girl as his keep called Sadaf. Verma Sahib and Agha Farhad exploit the girls and their singing talent. Later Agha Farhad marries 'a respectable girl' while Rushke Qamar suffers, having borne his illegitimate children. Their relationship, neatly summed up by the following conversation, replicates the power structure in their society:

> I know you too will desert me in a similar manner.
> Whichever girl your mother picks you shall marry that
> blessed youthful virgin princess (AJM, p.224).

Sadaf's accusation is met with Verma Sahib's anger:

> Look here Sadaf don't irritate me. Go and sleep. Have
> you forgotten what you were? Look how I have changed

> your destiny. I have turned you into a famous artist. Be satisfied and do not dream impossible dreams. I transformed an obscure street singer into Sadaf Ara Begum. But you are still cribbing (AJM, p.224)."

A comparison of the discourse used by Verma Sahib with that of Sadaf's reflects power and powerlessness respectively. By using terms like 'blessed', 'youthful', 'virgin', and 'princess' Sadaf expresses all that she is not and that which the male society wants her to be. Verma can love her as long as Sadaf shows her gratefulness to him. He must always put her in her place; the class barrier should not be transgressed. One can see here an alliance between patriarchy and aristocracy.

In Bond's novella Ruth and her mother Mariam discover that the women in the Pathan household, though living a subjugated and obscure existence, have an identity of their own. In the Muslim households –men swore, fought, and took wives of their own will without paying heed to what the women in the household felt. The women were supposed to be subservient yet Khan Begum(his wife)had her way in preventing Javed from marrying Ruth, the English girl. On their visit to the households of the relatives of Javed, Ruth and her mother realize (to their great relief) that none of the women are supportive of his intention to marry Ruth. They also learn about Qamran's (Javed's sister) dominance and control in her household. She is quick to condemn Umda, another family member for her rudeness to Mariam and Ruth. Mariam finds love, attention and respect amidst the household women because she possesses the qualities that they value. She is skilled in sewing, is well versed in herbs, folk remedies and folk tales and above all is forbearing. It is through these qualities that she is able to gel with the women in Qamran's household. The women in the household in their turn readily sympathize with Mariam for all the travails that she has been through. It can be argued that though Mariam and Ruth belong to the British patriarchal set up and the problems facing British and Indian women are vastly different, yet in some way both British and Indian women are a subjugated lot and hence there is an easy and smooth forming of relationships between them in *A Flight of Pigeons.* The women in Muslim households are not lacking in intellectual powers and political awareness, even though news of the outside world reaches them after long intervals of time. Thus Kothiwali's (another of Javed's relatives) comments on Javed's association with the rebellion of 1857 touch not only her 'experience' at the hands of the English but also her sympathies for innocent women and children, be they Indian or British:

> 'I wonder why your sympathies are with them, Chachi?' 'Well, they have always been quite good to me,' she replied….At the same time, don't think I wish to run down the cause you have made your own—the rebel cause, I mean. 'The *rebel* cause! Why do you always call it the rebel cause, Chachi?' Javed looked very upset. 'Rebels against whom? Against aliens! Are they not to be expelled from the land? To fight them is not rebellion, but a meritorious act, surely!' "Maybe, if it doesn't involve the murder of innocent women and children….. (Kothiwali replied) (FP, p.877)

A similar sense of togetherness, sympathy and love can be discerned between the three women in Hyder's story as the tragic stories of their lives unfold. However, there is a marked difference in the two stories in terms of the status of women characters. In *A Flight of Pigeons* the women belong to a prosperous household and for all the discrimination against them, are protected by the men folk. In Hyder's story they aspire for security, wish to get out of the clutches of poverty and want to marry and become respectable. But as street singers they are only playthings in the hands of exploiting men who don the garb of protectors and friends to ferry them towards security and prosperity. Jamilan who is crippled in the legs fights to live a respectable existence and sings with her sister. Rushke Qamar, after having been betrayed by Agha Farhad, falls in love with an Iranian who she says promised to marry her.

Her sister Jamilan's concern in this regard is reflective of their sense of togetherness and their commitment to each other:

> "Bajia—is this Agha Hamdani really prepared to marry you?"
>
> "He has said so clearly."

"It appears that you have fallen in love with him. He is certainly very handsome."

"Yes, I have fallen in love with him— I have never ever fallen in love before. I'm crazy about him and he loves me greatly too."

"But I am not convinced that he will call you to Karachi or London and marry you."

"Don't cast an evil eye on my happiness. You are jealous of my happiness—you lame witch" (AJM, p.226).

But Jamilan's fears are not unfounded. Agha Hamdani deserts Rushke Qamar who later gives birth to his daughter Maah Paara. Sadaf and Jamilan support her as she awaits the return of Agha Hamdani. Rushke Qamar writes letters to Agha Hamdani that are never answered and visits all sorts of faith healers and squanders all her savings. Verma Sahib too deserts Sadaf and marries a wealthy girl. The lame Jamilan is a witness to all this as the three of them support each other in whatever way they can. Ultimately for the future of teenaged Maah Paara, Rushke Qamar undertakes an arduous journey to Karachi, intending to meet Agha Hamdani.

The letters that Jamilan and Rushke Qamar write to each other during this period are never received by either, but they show the reader the trials and tribulations that the three women undergo; the Song Bird's Club closes after Verma Sahib's marriage and puts an end to Jamilan and Sadaf's meager income of fifty rupees. Sadaf ultimately marries a wealthy American. Jamilan and her aunt are left to fend for themselves. Jamilan refuses any monetary support from Sadaf or Agha Farhad. Even though she is lame, she manages to earn her living by doing *chikan* work.

Looking at Kothiwali or Khan Begum in Bond's story and Jamilan and Rushke Qamar in Hyder's story would suggest that in the patriarchal set up their life is a struggle. However, it can be argued, that despite their suffering these women display great courage, patience, and a fiery tenacity. When the men of Javed's family learn that the revolt has been quelled in Delhi and hear about the impending approach of the British in Shahjahanpur, Kothiwali takes the lead, displaying rare skills of leadership and confidence:

> And so Kothiwali, who had remained quietly at home all through the most violent stages of the revolt, now showed her qualities as a leader. She ordered these rough, disorderly men about as though they were children, and brought about a sense of organization where otherwise panic might have prevailed (FP, p.888).

Likewise Rushke Qamar displays rare courage and perseverance when she reaches Karachi with her daughter. She takes up the job of a housemaid. Her beautiful daughter, lured by the desire for riches, takes up modelling and begins to keep company with rich foreigners. Rushke Qamar's refusal to give up her humble profession causes embarrassment to her daughter and estranges them from each other. Even though Rushke Qamar began life as a poor humble street singer, she is not tempted by glamour or riches to give up her values.

When Maah Paara is murdered and Rushke Qamar is summoned to the police station, her answer to questions reveal she has finally realized that she is alone and that Agha Hamdani will never return. Rushke Qamar manages to go back to her home, hoping to find solace in the company of Jamilan. She finds that Jamilan is dead, and she still has to struggle for her livelihood in the most respectable manner possible. She is too old to sing. She picks up the only hope of a respectable living and that is *chikan* work.

In Bond's story too, though Ruth and Mariam were captives in Javed's household, they display their loving feelings and sincere emotions at the time of parting. The unconditional love and warmth in Javed's household won them over. Though in the eyes of Javed and other men, Ruth and her family belonged to the side of the oppressors, between the women no such distinction seemed to exist. The women of Javed's household treated them without any distinction in mind. Interestingly enough, Mariam and Ruth identify themselves with the Muslim women so much that when the British forces are coming to Shahjahanpur, they decide to flee with Javed's family. The following lines are pertinent to quote in this regard:

> Yes,' said Mother, 'for how will they know us for what we are? We have no one among them who would receive and protect us. From our complexions and our clothes they would take us for Mohammedan women, and we will receive the same treatment as your women. No, for present we are identified with you all, and we must go where you go (FP, p.888).

Bond has thus presented a warm and enduring picture of women in a Muslim household as seen through the eyes of the British and has not supported any stance of superiority of culture on the British side.

In Hyder's story too, the hidden strength of women is brought out in a rigidly male dominated society. This is specially so in the case of Jamilan who was lame and terminally ill. Her meager earnings of rupees twenty a month through *chikan* work were not enough to keep body and soul together.

Bafati, the poor rickshaw puller, who was by her side in her last moments, says:

> So long as she could move about she sang songs for radio. When she became bed-ridden she began to do *chikan* work. She would earn twenty rupees. She died of starvation. We would share our meager ration of food with her but I know she used to go without food and would remain hungry. She would say 'do not starve your wife and children for my sake.' She used to take a bite or two and then retire saying that she was suffering from indigestion. She would drop off to sleep while doing *chikan* work in the light of a lantern (AJM, p.255).

The lines quoted above adequately illustrate the dignity in the character of Jamilan. As the story closes Rushke Qamar too must tread the path that her sister left behind because she too is a victim in a male dominated society.

Notes and References

1. Ruskin Bond, *A Flight of Pigeons* in *Ruskin Bond: The Complete Short Stories and Novels* (New Delhi: Viking, 1996), p.849. (All subsequent references to *A Flight of Pigeons* are abbreviated as FP and are indicated by page numbers only.)

2. Qurratulain Hyder, 'Agle Janam Mohe Bitia Na Kijo' in *Qurratulain Hyder Ki Muntakhab Kahaniyan* (India: National Book Trust,1995), p.205. (All subsequent references to 'Agle Janam Mohe Bitia Na Kijo' are abbreviated as AJM and indicated by page numbers only.) I have myself translated the passages quoted from the Urdu original.

3. K.K. Ruthven, *Feminist literary studies: An Introduction* (New York: Cambridge University Press, 1984) p.95.

Chapter - 8

A Muslim Woman's Life in Qurratulain Hyder's Fiction with Special Reference to *Sita Betrayed*, *The Housing Society* and *A Woman's Life.*

Humera Khatoon

Qurratulain Hyder (b. 1927) entered the world of creative writing when radical changes in the form of political revolution were uprooting the traditional values and culture, of which the byproduct was the emergence of a new society. The Zamindari system, to which Hyder belonged, stood abolished. And the upheaval that took place at the time of Partition directly affected her and provoked her to raise certain questions with regard to the new emerging society with new values on human relationships. It is the culture of the spirit, which gains prime importance in her writings. The repertoire of her novels, novelette and short stories is rich and needs special attention. She has written seven novels, four novelettes, eight collections of short stories, two-volumes family saga and several translations. Her *The Sound of Falling Leaves* is the recipient of the Sahitya Akademi award. The two novelettes and one novel with which we are concerned here are - *Sita Betrayed* (1960), *The Housing Society* (1963), and *The Nautch Girls.* The tone of all the three stories is extremely pessimistic on account of the tragic fate, which meets the female characters. Being a woman herself, Hyder understands and deals sensitively with the problems of women.

The title of Qurratulain Hyder's *Sita Betrayed* is indicative of the theme of the novella – i.e. Sita's betrayal by all men who come in her life. Sita Mirchandani is a Hindu refugee from Sindh. The way she trusts others leads to her betrayal as well as torment. On the whole she is an extremely sensitive person with an inquisitive mind. This is how Sita's character is defined:

> It was only Sita's crazy mind that kept constantly asking questions about religion, about politics, about death and life and everything else in the world.[1]

This remark suggests that her mental make-up is a bit different from ordinary people who pay little heed to deeper philosophical questions of life and death.

There is deep emptiness, which engulfs Sita's personality. She is a poor creature, always in search of peace and comfort and tries to seek it in every nook and corner. The reason for her emotional attachment with Hima's house is that the place has always given her an abundant feeling of peace and security. She compares with surprise the peaceful life of Hima with her shattered world. She admits:

> For her this house was still like a safe and quiet ship anchored in a harbour, every once in a while she came here to harmonize herself to its peace" and then questions herself "Is so much peace possible[2]?

Sita Betrayed does not directly deal with the event of Partition yet the resonance of Partition in the story is palpable. Sita is a victim of Partition. The migration of her family has worsened their economic condition to such an extent that it could never again regain its lost position. Owing to his illness her father could not continue his clinical practice in an alien land while her mother could not come to terms with the loss of the glory of bygone days. Therefore one observes that although Partition is not directly discussed, its devastating effects are writ large on some of the major characters. For Sita it is a matter of great humiliation to invite her friends to her decrepit house. Sita argues vehemently with Bilqis:

> Bilqis – Hima lives in a fancy house. How can I invite her to my place? I don't even have enough space to sit. You are my relative, with you it doesn't matter.[3]

Before Partition Sita had lived in Sindh in a splendid house but the tragedy of 1947 has changed her economic condition. It hurts her pride to let her high profile friends see her present impoverished condition.

The name 'Sita' evokes the picture of a *Sati-Savitri* kind of a woman who is fully devoted and faithful to her husband. But Sita Mirchandani stands at the other extreme. She is never satisfied with one man. The reason behind her dissatisfaction is that she wishes to maintain an ideal relationship with her man in whom she could confide totally. All these men who enter her life appear to be very reliable but when she starts living with them; their true colours are revealed to her. Sita of the *Ramayana* was betrayed only by one Ravana but the modern Sita is in a worse situation. She is preyed upon mercilessly by a group of Ravanas. Qurratulain Hyder has tried to show mirror to the society, which is dominated by hollow and faithless men - Jamil, Irfan, Projesh Kumar, Qamrul Islam Chowdhry who cannot be put in the category of villains. In the eyes of the world they are the cream of society – a group of intellectuals. But if we observe them we find that in reality they are a product of a valueless society and therefore cannot be trusted. They are all empty from within. Being a product of the same vainglorious and immoral society, Sita is also not much different from others. But what makes her special is her sensitivity. She intensely cares for the feelings of others. Mercy and sympathy are at the core of her being. If, at times, she acts immorally then it is also out of her deep felt sympathy towards others. Her illicit relationship with Projesh Kumar and Qamrul Islam Chowdhry prove this. It is not an evil in Sita which constantly impels her to let men gather around her. On the contrary it is basically the motherly instinct in Sita that urges her to do so. Without taking into consideration the serious impact of such actions she keeps on moving from one man to another. If someone approaches her, seeking her company, she never returns him disappointed.

Sita is also daring and courageous. She is not like others who consider themselves as very pure, honest and find fault with others. Sita is bold enough to critically analyze her own self. While talking to Irfan about Jamil's rejection of her plea for the custody of Rahul, she says that Jamil considers her 'morally unfit to be a mother of an innocent child' and then she confesses: "And, you know Irfan, perhaps he was right on that score. At least in the eyes of the world….."[4] Her acceptance of guilt makes her worthy of respect and sympathy and raises her stature morally.

Hyder also brings into light one of the bitter truths that generally men take women for granted. Usually it is a woman who tries hard for a smooth relationship in a family. Although Jamil was deeply in love with Sita before marriage but things changed rapidly thereafter. He soon loses interest in her and starts spending much time in pubs. It is to some extent his negligence towards Sita which drives her into the arms of Qamrul Islam Chowdhry. If Sita is responsible for betraying her husband which she honestly admits: "I was in fact drawing closer to Qamar just the way a snake's prey is pulled closed to the snake."[5] Jamil too, cannot be exonerated. The first step towards breaking down the relationship was taken by him and not by Sita. She shares her pain with Irfan:

> No girl could have changed herself as much as I did to adapt to Jamil's ways. I even began to drink a lot so that I could keep him company in the evenings. But whenever I tried to accompany him to a bar he got angry; "Can't you leave me alone for even a minute", he would shout at me.[6]

Sita appears to be a modern and liberal kind of woman. It is no doubt true that anybody will get deceived by her extravagant outward behavior but from within she is totally different. It is her ardent wish to live like a typical devoted Indian woman who is all love and care for her husband. Her life in Jamil's house and her short stay with Irfan in Paris makes it clear. At both the places she had deeply involved herself with the little household chores, at the expense of her academic career:

> Irfan had found a lovely flat close to Boulevard Souchet, which Sita furnished and made lovelier still. Every morning Irfan would go off to his office while Sita would go and buy groceries. She would prepare the food, iron the clothes, clean the house, and put Irfan's slippers by his armchair near the fireplace for his return.[7]

Through Sita's conduct the author seems to hint at a vital point that sacrifices should not be expected only from women but from men too. If she commits any mistake, she should be given at least one opportunity to mend her ways. Jamil, in a fit of wild rage, throws her out of his house when he comes to know of her infidelity. But if she were given a chance, she would have certainly made amendments. It is ironical that such generosity is hardly expected of men. Sita confides in Irfan:

> When Jamil pushed me out of his house, I stood on the sidewalk in the rain for quite sometime. If he had then opened his door and said - just once-'Sita, come in out of the rain', I'd have the thrown myself at his feet and sworn never to be unfaithful again. But the door remained shut.[8]

Sita's constant search for a life partner suggests that a woman is always in search of a mental companion in the form of a husband who could provide her with mental as well as physical security of a peaceful home. C.M. Naim comments:

> Sita Mirchandani in *Sita Betrayed*, despite betrayals by a series of men, must remain alive to her own essentially felt need: it is as if, for her, ceasing to search for a shared and lasting experience of love would mean self annihilation.[9]

Hyder's stories depict the evil of modern society – a society which has gradually become devoid of basic human values. Such a society of loose moral values has turned men merely into pleasure-seeking creatures. Materialism has taken hold of society and little place is left for tender and noble emotions and sentiments. All these effects have driven man away from true happiness and made him restless. Sita is an intelligent woman who can look through such stark realities. She suffers more because she is highly sensitive. Her soul in distress wanders from place to place in search of genuine love. In her journey of life many men come but none could satisfy her thirsty soul; they took her as a mere plaything. She remembers with pain what Projesh Kumar had once said to her:

> Sita Debi, you're such a strange girl. You'll have a hard time finding happiness in this world – the kind of happiness you seem to desire.[10]

To a certain degree Projesh Kumar is right in his assessment of Sita that she will always suffer in order to find happiness. But she cannot be put into the category of 'strange' people. She is a normal and plain woman who wishes to lead a happy and contented life. But the modern world around her has become devoid of good human beings due to which she has to struggle hard. So one can say that Sita is not strange, the world around her has become strange. And such a selfish world is enough to kill a sensitive and emotional woman like Sita. *Sita Betrayed* is written by a woman from a woman's point of view. It seems as if Hyder is warning women against the tyrannical world around them.

Sita is a curious amalgam of practical wisdom and emotions. Irfan points towards this aspect of her personality: "You put so much value on sentiments.... Yet you claim to be so very logical. What a fraud you are!"[11]. It is not an abnormal feature of Sita if there is improper balance between sentiments and logic in her personality. To be emotional is something natural in her and to be logical is the demand of her society. The battle between the two keeps on going within her for which she cannot be held responsible. Therefore to call her a fraud due to these qualities is unjust.

Sita has formed two separate worlds of her own. One is the outside world in which she acts mostly in accordance with the needs and desires of others. Her own self becomes secondary in this world which she keeps on surrendering unhesitatingly to the will of men. Projesh Kumar, Qamrul-Islam Chowdhry and others exploit her emotionally. However, Sita is not a fool who does not understand their ways of trapping her. She sees through all this but cannot check that natural instinct in her which knows only to give and to sacrifice. She recalls one such incident:

> That night in the Constitution House, Projesh had said to her, 'Sita Debi, I have lived an extremely lonely life. The world understands my paintings, but it doesn't understand me .....' So many beautiful girls came into my life, Sita

> Debi, but none could look into the depths of my soul."
> Sita knew Projesh was putting on a big act, but that only served to make her pity him. Projesh would often say to her, child-like, "I need you, Sita Debi", and the mother in Sita would come awake.[12]

The other world is the interior world of her lonely heart in which she lives with all her sorrows and disappointments. In such a dreary world she has no companion. Sita realizes with horror:

> In this world, in this huge sprawling, glittering capital, in the midst of a crowd of acquaintances, she had no one to share her sorrow. Why? Why was it so? She hadn't hurt anyone.[13]

Sita is a poor victim of Partition. She had lost her home in Karachi during those turbulent days. After many years when she comes back to Karachi, she gets very emotional. An element of nostalgia is evident in her voice when she shares with Irfan her childhood incidents: "Look over there. You see that tree? When we'd go to Hyderabad we'd always stop under it to rest. Once I hurt my leg badly....."[14]

At Sadhbela gloom descends upon her when she sees with pain the writings of those people in the temple who had to run away during Partition riots. There is a deep feeling of depression which time and again keeps engulfing her lonely self. At Sadhbela her frustration reaches its climax:

> How dark it is! And in this darkness all my ideals, all my longings and regrets glow faintly – like will –o' –the wisps. Just now, when I closed my eyes for a moment, I felt as if Bhairon's dog had attacked me and I couldn't escape because I was surrounded by witches riding hyenas.[15]

It is horror of living alone which wounds and bleeds her heart, changing her loyalties at different turns of her life. If she keeps on shifting her stance at various stages of life, she should not be blamed. It is basically the fault of her society, which has groomed such individuals who are unable to safeguard the honor of a woman and provide her with lifetime security.

Sita always feels isolated and betrayed. Her relationship with every male ends up in a doom, making her more isolated than before. Finally when Irfan marries, without letting her even know, she is completely broken: "Sita's voice sounded as if it came from the bottom of a deep well"[16]. Her inner voice speaks to her: "All my life long I've been preyed upon"[17]. This comes out to be the ultimate truth of her tragic life.

Sita Betrayed ends on a deep note of pessimism. Through Sita's character Hyder has shown that this world is a mere illusion and everybody is running after a mirage. At the end of the journey what they get is utter disappointment and failure.

The Housing Society

Qurratulain Hyder belonged to landed gentry and her experience of the traditional environment of the village is very personal and therefore close to her heart. She treats with sympathy the life of the villagers. But she makes no effort to hide her dislike for the neo-rich business class, which has shattered traditional values. She seems to believe that as a result of this breakdown a valueless society has come into being which cares little for the sentiments of the people and judges people according to their financial position. In *The Housing Society,* Hyder brings into contrast the pre-Partition culture with the post-Partition one. Cultural deterioration is her favourite theme, which she discusses in an objective manner.

Housing Society is a posh residential area in the city of Karachi. Mainly highflying business-class families live there. *The Housing Society* takes into account the stories of three families. One is of Jamshed who is a refugee from the village Muhammad Ganj, Distt Sultanpur, India. Jamshed spent his early life in India under impoverished conditions but his desire to become a wealthy man gets fulfilled after he migrates to Pakistan. His hard labour brings success and money together in his life. He also cleverly hides the poor economic background of his family and poses to be of high lineage in India. However, in reality he is a son of a simple cultivator in India. Jamshed belongs to that neo- rich class that feels ashamed of its poor family background.

The other strand of the story includes Surayya who also belonged to the class of commoners. When young she experienced the pains of abduction and fought a long battle in the court against her abductors. Her father was an ordinary cultivator. Like Jamshed she also arrives in Karachi in a state of wilderness but soon gains popularity owing to her natural talents of an artist. The introductory note about her as an artist after her arrival in Karachi in the newspaper report reveals that how she has distorted the truth in order to make a new identity of herself:

> Miss Husain, whose father was a prominent landholder in Uttar Pradesh (India) was educated in a convent school in Mussoorie and after that at Santiniketan.[18]

Salman–Salma's episode runs parallel to the above plots and intermingles with the other two. The good fortune of Salma's family declines after Partition. The family condition further deteriorates when Salma's brother is jailed. He is shown as a revolutionary who wants to fight for the cause of equality of all in his land. Though Hyder has not discussed explicitly the subject of Partition in *The Housing Society*, its strong impact can be felt. For instance, the scene in which Salman seeks out his family in Karachi is heart-wrenching. He is shocked to see his family in a pitiable condition – the family which had always enjoyed the fruits of comfort, wealth and power is now in want and misery. Salman's father becomes bed-ridden and lack of money worsens his condition. His sister Choti Bitiya, who had always lived a carefree and luxurious life, is suddenly burdened with family responsibilities. She has to pick up a job in a school as a teacher and abandon her academic career. While depicting the disastrous after-effects of Partition, Hyder has shown this world as a place of never-ending pain and continuous struggle.

In *The Housing Society* Hyder has made an attempt to focus on the striking difference between the traditional village life and the ultra-modern city life. Jamshed and her sister, Aliya, are truly representative of that neo-class that has completely forgotten its roots. The glittering and shimmering lights of the city have engulfed them completely. Jamshed becomes a successful businessman - well equipped with nasty business tricks. The high ideals of honesty, morality and loyalty have no place in his world. He feels no shame in accepting that like others he is also actively involved in black-marketing and is one of the members of the society that follows the 'rule of the jungle'. In a letter to Salma he confesses:

> Today's world is a great, big black market. Here intellects and minds and hearts and souls are bought and sold. I've seen big name artists and intellectuals, believers and non-

> believers, all being sold for a price. I myself often trade in them.[19]

Jamshed involves himself in expanding his business and in making contacts to such an extent that he even forgets that he is a father of a little girl and has some responsibilities towards her. It is after so many years that he goes to meet her and then decides to bring her with him. By temperament his sister, Aliya, is more or less like him – a product of the same materialistic society. In letters to his uncle in the village she would try to impress him with her rising standard of life:

> Today, Bhayya bought a new car. By the grace of God, it cost forty thousand rupees. Yesterday, Bhayya left for Europe on a business trip. This is his fourth trip to Europe. Next month I'm going to New York. It is a very large city in America.[20]

Aliya seems to take delight in describing her life of pomp and show to her poor relatives.

In contrast to Aliya and Jamshed are the village folks who are comparatively very simple and sober. Syed Mazhar Ali, Jamshed's uncle, along with the group of other villagers welcomes Jamshed with open arms. He has no feeling of hatred against his nephew for having ruined the life of his only daughter, Manzurun Nisa, whom he loves more than anything. Hyder appears to suggest that the neo-rich class gives more importance to wealth than to values while the people embracing old values carry the spirit of sacrificing everything for the sake of strengthening the bond of human relationships. The manner in which the entire village shares the responsibility of Jamshed's daughter is amazing. Syed Mazhar Ali tells Jamshed about the academic progress of the child: "I myself teach her Urdu and the Holy Quran. Shambhu Bhayya teaches her the A,B,C,D. Gosain Bhayya is teaching her Hindi, Syed Mazhar Ali proudly told him."[21]

The new house of Jamshed is a den of moral degradation. The different types of people, especially business magnates are representative of the new emerging bourgeoisie class. Jamshed spends money extravagantly on the party in order to make more and more contacts and create an impression of his overflowing wealth. There is wine, obscenity and vulgarity all there. People are shown having fights on petty business matters.

As in *Sita Betrayed* most of the men exploit Sita for their own purpose, so does happen to women characters in *The Housing Society* as well. Jamshed, an extremely opportunist person, treats women according to his fancy. Three women come in his life. The first one is his wife whom he maltreated because she never raised her voice and regarded her husband as next to God. Finally he divorces her, considering her as an incompetent life-partner. The second woman who enters his life is Salma. She was a member of the class highly respected and held in great esteem before 1947, owing to its immense power and wealth. In those times Jamshed, whose father was a mere farmer, could not even dare dream of standing together with Collector sahib's family. When Salma's family migrates to Pakistan, their entire property is confiscated and declared as 'evacuee property'. At this point Hyder shows fate playing strange tricks when Salma unknowingly becomes his secretary. Something even unthinkable happens accidentally without Jamshed's own realization of the reality. Though Salma is exceptionally beautiful and Jamshed could have thought of marrying her in a decent manner but again his meanness impels him to use her cunningly for his business purpose instead of marrying her. While dismissing the idea of marriage he thinks:

> What nonsense am I thinking? What marriage? Whose marriage? I shall groom this girl. She'll prove to be an excellent 'contact' person. Even the wiliest crook will fall for her innocent face and spill out business secrets. Business worth millions will be settled in minutes.....[22]

The third woman whom he finally accepts to be his wife is Surayya – an artist of world fame. When she migrated to Karachi there were other goals in her mind. The major one being the search of Salman, her lover, whom she had loved dearly and passionately. While waiting for Salman, Surayya's innocent desire was to paint her pictures in the latter's presence.

In a state of bewilderment she questions herself: "Will the day come when we'll be together and I'll paint pictures of these forests and rivers in your presence?"[23] With Salman's life-time imprisonment their relationship comes to an abrupt end. If Jamshed decides to marry her, there must be certain reasons behind it. The main objective appears to be Surayya's popularity as an artist that would facilitate his business. This is why he finally selects Surayya as his wife. Hence, we find that the lives of the three women characters are shaped and controlled by one single man. This indirectly reflects the worthlessness of women in the patriarchal society.

Surayya fits perfectly in the framework of a modern woman who knows well how to keep pace with the fast moving world – the world in which one has to strive in order to make some room. Basanti Begum alias Surayya struggles hard in order to survive. The atmosphere of Karachi brings incredible changes in Surayya's personality. She transforms herself according to the demands of time. The same Surayya who was extremely simple – an ideal of Salman – becomes a highly fashionable woman of the day. She starts wearing make-up, revealing dresses, and drinking wine like most of the fashionable women: "…She was now 'someone' and couldn't just go out in ordinary clothes. Her standard of living was constantly rising and getting more expensive."[24] It is sad that the woman whom Salman had always idealized gets lost in the maddening crowd of the city. To some extent she succeeds, at least in the eyes of the world. Like her, Salma also leads a life of toil. Although she does not fully achieve the fruits of her hard labour, the continuous attempts, which she makes, are worth noting. In contrast to these two women is a minor character - Manzurun Nisa. As she keeps on accepting hardships without protest, Jamshed is able to exploit her. She enters his life in the form of a compromise and moves out, making herself a burden on her parents. The most important characteristic of Hyder's major female characters is their will to survive and not to surrender. Their struggle is continuous; no matter whether they win or lose.

Ms. Hyder laments the lost glory of bygone days – how the new emerging class has crushed the dignity and honour of the former ruling class. One feels the sharpness of irony in her representation – the kind of sadness in tone which comes only as a result of some personal grief or loss.

One observes marked similarity between Attia Hosain's and Qurratulain Hyder's depiction of the effects of Partition. In Hosain's *Sunlight on a Broken Column* the picture of the abolition of the *Zamindari* system strikes a sad note. Asad, Laila's cousin, had once told Laila: "The ugliness is inevitable, when palaces are pulled down and mud huts are exposed to view it is not a pleasant sight. There is rubble and dust in any demolition."[25] We hear echoes of Asad's voice in Salman's words in *The Housing Society* when he tells Surayya: "The mansions of the past have burned down, but the mansions of the new bourgeoisie will soon rise on their debris in both countries. Yesterday's feudal lords will give way to today's Capitalists."[26] Time proves the predictions of both Asad and Salman to be true; it is ironical that the desire of the rise of bourgeoisie class results in the deprivation of their own families. While dealing with the Partition problem, there seems to be a common ground between Qurratulain Hyder and Attia Hosain. Both the novelists have expressed their desire to strengthen personal ties and they felt a sort of pain when they were broken.

When a man lives an evil life without any moral scruples, he can carry on with the business of life satisfactorily. However, things become miserable if the sense of guilt starts torturing him. Hyder has presented a world in which most of the characters appear to have accepted the superficial kind of life they are leading. But the reader is shocked to realize that a dim spark of remorse still exists in their hearts. Jamshed's letter to Salma towards the end brings the realization that he who appears to be insensitive is in reality aware of his own hollowness and deceit. Similarly Surayya appears to have forgotten Salman but it is not so. Salman is in her heart: "Surayya clamped her eyes shut and whispered to herself, "Salman...you should forgive me too. Wherever you are...do please forgive me. Don't let me die like this..."[27] Surayya's quiet acceptance of Jamshed's proposal rests on a big compromise which she has to make in order to survive in this hypocritical world. We may conclude that Hyder has presented a world in which human beings are helplessly trapped and from which there is no escape. Either willingly or unwillingly they have to accept the crooked pattern of life. There is not much choice left to them. Hyder does not take her characters from the fairy tale world. They are neither saintly nor villains. Strictly speaking, they are normal, average human beings with their strengths as well as weaknesses.

A Woman's Life

Qurratulain Hyder's *A Woman's Life* is a study of the position of women in a patriarchal society. Gender discrimination, common in India, serves as a background theme in most of her novels. She indicates how certain attributes of chastity and purity have been associated with woman. If she fails to behave in accordance with these attributes, she is declared to be a fallen woman. But it is ironical that when men commit the same sins, they are hardly reproached by society. Hyder's work points to the victimization of women at all levels – be it in the educated middle class, illiterate lower class or the upper class.

Hyder's *A Woman's Life* is about two cousin sisters who gradually gain popularity as singers after having led a long life of penury. One of the sisters, Rashke Qamar, who is exceptionally beautiful, wavers after tasting a new life of luxury and comfort. Many men come in her life but none could provide her with a respectable status. She produces three children out of wedlock. The story ends, with her back to abject poverty. Her sister Jamila too, dies in impoverished conditions. The tragedy of the two sisters brings into focus the helplessness of woman in this world. Although Hyder's characters are not the passive receivers as they remain preoccupied constantly with hard struggle, yet what they achieve at the end of their journey is much below their expectations, which implies that often men and women are mere puppets in the hands of fate.

Helpless girls easily fall prey to the greed and lust of society. Rashke Qamar's beauty enchants at first Agha Farhad's lecherous father and then Farhad himself. Her exploitation is at all levels: i.e. within her own social circle as well as in the upper class which she enters with her new identity of an artist. When poor she was treated with disdain and contempt by her aunt Hurmuzi. Owing to want and hunger she had to bear the abuses hurled upon her by society. Considering her as a poor, helpless girl, others approached her with sinister designs in their minds. After attaining name and fame she was abused by the sophisticated and the "cultured people".

But it is ironic that her fate remains the same in both cases – her exploitation. More than her voice, it is her beauty which attracts others.

In *A Woman's Life* Jameela stands as a challenge to the world of men. Unlike her sister, she does not let men exploit her. She is a realistic person. Her sudden success, social upliftment and immense popularity do not turn her into a snob. On the contrary, it makes her extremely self-conscious. She tells Verma: "We have nothing but hardships and humiliations and all of a sudden our way of life has become so different. It makes me scared. It's too good to be true".[28] This statement in turn reflects the simplicity of her character. She emphatically asks Verma that the true background of the two sisters should be published in the magazine, *Gohar-i-Shab-Chiragh* and not the fake one invented by Verma. Her honesty disapproves all such falsehood. Jameela maintains her dignity and self-respect even on her deathbed. This is why she emerges as a strong character in the story. Like any other girl she too, has a heart bursting with desires, but her self-respect restrains her. In spite of physical deformity, she does not suffer from any sting of humiliation: "I am not ashamed". Your Almighty God was not ashamed of making such a sorry mess of our lives. But you watch out."[29] She accepts the ugliness of life calmly and without making any complaint. While her sister Rashke-Qamar stands in contrast with her as she abuses her beauty for infatuating men. Her relationships with Farhad and then Agha Shab Awaz are for securing her future. All these selfish motives bring her ill fame.

In *A Woman's Life* two sides of a woman can be seen. One side is of a highly ambitious woman who gives priority to the comforts of life and hence is materialistic as well as superficial in her attitude. The other is one who treats this world with a kind of detachment and gives more importance to the higher values of life. The luxuries of life do not hold any attraction for her. Jameela never begs anything; she never uses the money for her personal needs sent by Agha Farhad. She does not let herself to be a burden on anyone. Therefore, in spite of acute poverty, she is always treated with respect. Poverty could not rob her of self-respect, which is so dear to her. It is the effect of Jameela's strong personality, which provokes the poor rickshwala, her tenant, to exclaim:

> I know she died of hunger. After taking a few morsels she would say 'I have no appetite'. 'Or tummy upset. Can't eat anymore'. She felt she was a burden on us. She earned a few rupees through her embroidery. She would do her *chikan* work by the light of the lantern till midnight and then fall asleep. Isn't that the stuff saints are made of?[30]

Hyder has created Jameela's character with great care. Her profound sense creates a long lasting impression on readers. She pities uncle Jumman Khan who had loved the two sisters sincerely: "All his life the poor man has been jeered at and ridiculed. The One-Eyed Fool. The stupid Barber. The worthless mountebank. The world makes me sick".[31] Uncle Jumman is ridiculed because he is a petty pauper. The people around him due to his impoverished condition neglected the high qualities of his character. It is a bitter truth that in a modern world of today man is valued in accordance with his financial status. His wealth, rather than his values are reckoned often by the people. Rashke Qamar too, experiences such a cold attitude after she loses everything. Her poor condition receives little attention from her old time admirers. She reflects sadly upon Sheikh Taoos's conversation with her. Had she told him that she was staying at the Taj or at Oberoi – Shereton, he would have said: "I'm coming right away", or that "I'll come to fetch you myself or send you my car". Now he said a trifle coldly: "Oh, I see. All right… Do come over at about seven thirty or eight. You'll easily get a bus from Mohammad Ali Road. I live at Worli Seaface. Take down my address".[32] It reflects man's meanness; if one is a member of high class, he is highly respected by others and if not he is easily forgotten by society. All this implies that man as an individual has no importance in the social circle.

In spite of such a direct attack on the hollow values of society, Hyder does not show this world as a place full of complete darkness. If her writings show numerous untrustworthy persons, there are also many good ones too whose presence on the face of the earth promises good fortune.

In the novel characters like Maulvi Saheb, the Negishi family, and Mirza, Nanbai, are the ones who help Rashke Qamar without hoping for any reward and purely from a humane point of view. But unfortunately such selfless people are rare. However, their presence cannot be and should not be ignored as they give one confidence of living and make life worth living for other helpless beings.

Role of destiny remains at the center of Hyder's writings. The disappointments, which befall her struggling characters, suggest that everything is predestined, no matter how much one struggles. Sadaf Ara Begum, Verma's mistress, says sarcastically to Verma, her fortune maker: "Adopting a different name doesn't alter one's identity. You changed Jamila's name. Has it made any difference? She is still hobbling about, moping. I am a Hindu and you made me Sadaf Ara Begum. You call Jamil-un-Nissa 'Jalbala Lahiri'. How does it matter? Whatever is predestined, shall come to pass".[33]

Sadaf Ara and Rashke Qamar are victims of the deceit of men. In the beginning Verma talked eloquently about the cause of women. However, as the plot progresses we find that Verma's high-talk regarding women appears nothing but a facade - his hollow, superficial rantings. The way he forsakes Sadaf Ara, whom he had earlier kept in his house for love's sake, exposes his opportunistic nature. In order to save himself from bankruptcy, he makes an easy deal by marrying a wealthy woman. The love and sacrifice of a poor girl could not hold him from taking such a selfish decision. Verma breaks his twenty-five years of relationship with Sadaf Ara in an instant. Through such fickleness of men, Hyder points to the deterioration of society. On the one hand, she focusses upon the exploitation of women, then on the other, she also blames them unhesitatingly for their follies. Hence what emerges through her writings is not a sugar- coated image of a woman but the lively picture of flesh and blood. Such an image seems much nearer to reality. Rashke Qamar's sense of security, self-confidence and ambitions all are shattered under patriarchal pressures. Her lovers exploit her body but discard her after fulfilling their carnal desires. It is true that she has an immoral character due to which she suffers. But it is a pathetic question in the male-dominated society – that why only she is to live a life of loneliness and humiliation? Why are the men with whom she had illegal relationships allowed to live a respectable life? It is dissatisfying the way that men escape punishment. Hyder seems to criticize the patriarchal society, which places so much emphasis on women's chastity, irrespective of men's immorality. She portrays the trauma of being a woman – a petty picture of oppression and subjugation.

The mental make-up of Indian women is such that they hardly raise voice against injustices done to them. They are too timid to rebel against the supremacy of the male world. Rashke Qamar never claims the fatherhood of any one of her children and suffers all alone. The only thing she does is waiting. While remembering Rashke Qamar, Jamila recalls the tragic moments of her sister's life: "Seventeen long years my poor sister spent waiting to hear from him. Morning and evening she stood in the doorway looking out for the postman. Several times a day she asked me: Any letter? Any telegram? It was heart-breaking. What an incredibly long wait"![34]

On the one hand, Hyder's *A Woman's Life* is a witness to a woman's subjugation, oppression and defeat, and on the other, it is a challenging story of a woman's struggle to lead a dignified life in spite of extreme poverty. Here contrary images are found intermingling which focus on the multifaceted picture of a woman. Her remarkable approach to woman's tragedy shows her brilliant perception and understanding of human psychology.

To conclude, we may say that Hyder has painted the picture of contemporary society, which has freed itself from conventional morality. Although her female characters - Sita Mirchandani, Jameela and Surayya are seen defying the self-centeredness of the male world, their tragic end underscores, in a sense, the futility of their struggle.

Notes and References

1. Hyder, Qurratulain, (edited and introduced by C.M. Naim), *A Season of Betrayals: A Short Story and two Novellas*, New Delhi: Kali for Women, 1999, p.243.
2. Ibid., p.30
3. Ibid., p.46
4. Ibid., p.87
5. Ibid., p.84
6. Ibid., p.80
7. Ibid., p.160
8. Ibid., p.86
9. Ibid., p.165
10. Ibid., p.171
11. Ibid., p.165
12. Ibid., p.58
13. Ibid., p.71
14. Ibid., p.172
15. Ibid., p.172
16. Ibid., p.69
17. Ibid., p.XI (Introduction)
18. Ibid., p. 243
19. Ibid., p.265
20. Ibid., p.223
21. Ibid., p.222
22. Ibid., p.240
23. Ibid., p.224
24. Ibid., p.236
25. Attia Hosain, *Sunlight on a Broken Column*, London: Chatto and Windus 1961, pp.277-278.

26. *A Season of Betrayals: a short story and two novellas*, p.210.

27. Ibid., p.260

28. Hyder,Qurratulain, *A Woman's Life*, New Delhi: Chetna Publications, 1979, pp. 26-27.

29. Ibid., p. 27

30. Ibid., p.66

31. Ibid., p.32.

32. Ibid., p.53.

33. Ibid., p.34.

34. Ibid., p.38.

Chapter - 9

Muslim Women Characters in the Short Stories on Partition

Humera Khatoon

During perturbed times the greatest sufferers are invariably women. Lacking physical strength they usually become soft targets of the miscreants. The tale of their misery does not end just here but it drags them into the world of utter humiliation in spite of being innocent they are condemned by the society. The tragedies of victimized women during Partition days have been portrayed with vigour and pathos by many writers. For instance, Jameela Hashmi's 'Banished'[1], Syed Muhammad Ashraf's (b. 1957) ' Separated From the Flock[2], Kamleshwar's 'How Many Pakistans?'[3], Rajindar Singh Bedi's (b. 1920) 'Lajwanti'[4], Saadat Hassan Manto's (b. 1912) 'Mozel'[5] and Aziz Ahmad's (b. 1913) 'Kaali Raat'[6] are wonderful pieces of creative writings and give voice to the silent miseries of women. And fortunately enough, some of the stories have been translated into English - Umar Memon's collection *An Epic Unwritten* (1998) published by the Penguin Books, Alok Bhalla's *Stories about the Partition of India* came out in three volumes in 1994. Mushirul Hasan has also collected the translated stories of one of the volumes of *India Partitioned: the Other Face of Freedom* (1995)

Jameela Hashmi, a novelist and short story writer, was born in Lyallpur, Pakistan in 1929. She has produced several collections of short stories and many novels. Her most acclaimed novel *Talash-e-Baharan* was the recipient of the Adamjee Literary Award in Pakistan in 1960. Her other novel *Dasht-e Sus* (1983) is equally famous. *Aap-beeti, Jag-beeti* is a collection of her short stories. *Banished*, a popular

Partition story in Urdu, is taken from this collection which Mohammad Umar Memon has deftly translated into English.

Jameela Hashmi's 'Banished' is related to the theme of abduction and rape. In the story, the central character is a Muslim woman who has been abducted during Partition days by a Sikh and is compelled to live in his house as a housemaid and by whom she had two sons and one daughter. With the passage of time she develops a strong relationship with the mother of abductor. Though she laments present condition, yet she cannot dare leave the house: "Where can I go – with my wounded heart, my darkened fate? Munni stands in my way. She is the greater distance that separates me from my own family. How can I dare look beyond her, beyond that distance?"[7]

Rape is an unfortunate incident which can bring incredible changes in her relationship with others because in Indian society sexual purity of a woman determines her value at the most. It is ironical that the body of a mother (or woman in real sense) was brutally violated during Partition days. Many victimized women, unable to cope with the stigma of sexual impurity, ended their lives. Being the members of the same society they knew that they could never be forgiven for the crime in which they had no hand and were forcibly involved.

The narrator observes a great deal of similarity between her life and that of Sita. Just as Sita lived a banished life and bore the thorns of misery for no fault of her own, likewise the same tragedy befalls the narrator. The writer comments in this context: "Banishment is a hard thing to endure. But does one have control over anything? Anything at all? Who wants to suffer knowingly?"[8]

Sita (the mythical character of the epic, *Ramayna*) of the past, who had lived a life of banishment, was pure and was treated with respect and reverence. There was a great deal of dignity in her exile. But the present day Sita, i.e. the protagonist, is first raped and then forced to live all her life with the same person who had caused her this agony. In her exile what she receives back is insult and mental torture. M. Asaduddin comments:

> This Hindu myth that Jameela Hashmi takes recourse to (as do many other Muslim writers, like Intizar Hussain, Ashfaque Ahmad and Ghulam Abbas), along with the Dussehra celebrations, marking the destruction of Ravana, foregrounds a racial memory and a consciousness in which the tragedy of women cuts across religion and community.[9]

The status of a 'bahu' (daughter-in-law) that has been imposed on her is not real but false. How can she be given the place of a 'bahu' when, for her entire life, she remains unmarried? Traditionally feelings of affection and respect are associated with this particular word. But to her it appears like an insult as if someone has abused her: "Whenever anyone calls me 'bahu', I feel insulted. I have been hearing this word for years, ever since the evening when Gurpal dumped me in this courtyard and cried to Bari Ma, who was sitting on a Chauki. 'Look, Ma, I've brought you a bahu. A real beauty! The best of the lot!"[10]. The narrator's personality shatters under the heavy burden of the illegal title that has been imposed on her.

Jameela Hashmi's 'Banished' rests on the deep-felt consciousness of the female protagonist. The feeling of her separation from her family is so acute in her consciousness that she observes with great attention the little children who get lost on the eve of 'dussehra' (Hindu festival celebrating Rama's victory over Ravana). She could feel their pain because the same tragedy had befallen her also. Fate has mercilessly separated her from her dear ones: "Paths, like the watery webs etched on the waves by minuscule crawling marine life, dissolve behind us. We can never backtrack on the paths we have already taken. Nothing ever returns. And the milling, jostling crowd at the fair can only move forward."[11]

The misery of the protagonist is indeed pathetic. She considers herself as a lonely tree which neither blossoms nor bears fruit. She does not bloom as she has been uprooted from her natural surroundings and placed in an alien land. Gradually she has withered. She looks for the reflection of her life in those things that are devoid of life and forlorn: "A solitary star throbs forlornly in the sky, like flickering flame of an earthen lamp. In the blue empty space its loneliness reminds me of my banishment."[12] The kind of life she is living presently is totally different from the one she had spent earlier. There was love, comfort, dignity and sophistication in her past life. Her present stands in acute contrast with her past. Now she faces humiliation, loneliness, want, despair and submission. If outwardly she appears to be dutiful as well as respectful towards Gurpal's mother, it does not imply that she is satisfied with her present status. There is a volcano within her calm self that keeps smouldering within. Without complaining she performs entire household duties – churns milk, picks up the basketful of dung, makes cow-dung cakes with great effort, and does gorgeous embroidery. Her docile and submissive nature wins the heart of Bari Ma. The bonds between them become strong: "With time Bari Ma grew fond of me ... I'm her prized daughter-in-law now, her Lakshmi. She shows off the yarn spun by me to everyone she meets. When others complain about their daughter-in-law, she praises me to high heaven just to rub it in"[13]. She appears to be uncomplaining but in reality every pore of her body strongly revolts against the type of life she has been leading. And above all what can her complaints help her now? It will bring more disgrace to her, more beatings from Gurpal's mother. One makes complaints to those in whom one confides. How can she confide in her abductor the person who has deeply wounded her soul. Therefore she remains silent.

In 'Banished', Hashmi presents the intricate understanding between a mother and a daughter. Munni is so different from her mother, as her roots in the place, Sangroan, are stronger than those of her mother. An inexorable bond exists between Munni's body and the earth. Hashmi seems to point out that it is the effect of that bond which makes man complete from within. Munni is like that pear tree which is implanted in the courtyard of the house with its roots going deep below:

> The pear tree has blossomed every year since Munni was born. When the seasons change, its branches become filled with flowers, the tree bends over heavy with fruit, deepening its bond with the earth. Its roots burrow deeper into the soil. No one can rupture that bond. Man imbibes

> the culture of the place he lives in and his displacement creates a gap in his life and a feeling of never-ending pain.[14]

The style in which the story "Banished" has been written by Hashmi is striking for its intensity of pain. It evokes pathos and compassion. Each word of it seems to have sprung from a bleeding heart longing for mercy. The similes and metaphors that have been used in the story leave their imprint on the mind of the readers. For instance, "My heart was throbbing fitfully, like the lonely star trembling with apprehension above the blue mist in the clear western sky."[15] "...and the light of the receding ship flickered like a lonely star and then faded away/"[16]; "Hopes keep circling the heart like vagrant thoughts."[17]; "In this human wilderness I am like a lonely tree which neither blossoms nor bear fruit."[18] The morbid story of Partition has been depicted by Hashmi when friends turned into foes and the country rolled into the fire of hatred. Those who had put their faith in humanity were let down. The narrator sarcastically recalls the biggest tragedy of her life in tears:

> Well, maybe Bhai and Bhaiyya weren't present at my Wedding – so what? Hadn't Gurpal rolled out a carpet of corpses for me? Painted the roads red with blood? Provided an illumination by burning down city after city? Didn't people celebrate my wedding as they stampeded, screaming and crying?[19]

Partition of the country came as a shock to the entire nation. A country which had been brought together over a period of time and enriched culturally got divided by those who were essentially behind its making. When a woman like Hashmi's protagonist is abducted and bound to live a life of humiliation, it results in the creation of a crippled nation. What sort of values can a morally corrupt father and an emotionally bankrupt mother impart to their children? The differences by religion and the politics of Partition blinded the masses, turning them out of their wits. In this context Hashmi comments:

> The face of everything, was covered with blood. The very people who did charity in the name of Bhagwan,

> Guru and Allah slaughtered each other, those who readily laid down their lives to save the virtue of their sisters and daughters considered a woman's honour no more than an illusion.[20]

The dividing line between reality and illusion gets dissolved for the narrator when events take a drastic turn in her life. Earlier the greatest reality of her existence used to be her family but now the same reality has subsided into an illusion. The faces of her dear ones have become part of her memory and are now no more real. She feels that "Outside Sangraon, all other villages look like doll houses to me, devoid of reality. Perhaps Sangraon too is unreal, a mere shadow. Perhaps everything is just a shadow."[21] Instead of giving emphasis on horrifying details Hashmi focuses on some of the universal truths faced by man in day-to-day life.

In Hashmi's 'Banished' hope gives way to despair. For years the protagonist keeps on entertaining the hope of meeting her family. But the dim light of that flickering hope finally diminishes. Hence Partition becomes a metaphor for a tortured soul as millions of people suffered on account of it. Her anxiety is crystal clear in this passage: "The thought crossed my mind that perhaps Bhai and Bhaiyya too, would come looking for me. They must have waited long for me outside the gates of the magic city .... Everyday I'd tie my hopes into a bundle and peer with anticipation and longing at the bend in the lane."[22]

Hashmi portrays the repressed self of a woman through her protagonist in the story. She endures Gurpal's insult as well as the beatings of his mother without a word of complaint because somewhere in the deep corner of her heart a ray of hope persists that someday her Bhaiyya and Bhai would come to Sangraon and take her along. And then 'wind would rustle through the neem leaves and sing and the entire village would celebrate and rejoice.'[23] Though she hates to live a life of such humiliation in Gurpal's house but she has no other option. Hashmi's female character is totally dependent on her male counterpart. She waits impatiently for her brothers and when they do not come, she refuses to leave Gurpal's home and go along with the soldiers who come for the repatriation of abducted women during Partition. Finally the beauty of the past gets dissolved in the ugliness of the present. That beautiful home of her past life which she had nurtured so lovingly gets shattered. Rodh Prakash, a critic, opines: "Both these strands come together in the narrator's consciousness, and while the past is clearly more desirable than the present, there is also an acute consciousness that it is irrecoverable."[24]

Another reason which Hashmi provides to her narrator for deciding to stay in Sangraon all her life is that slowly with time her roots have sunk deep in the place. With the birth of Munni her bond with Sangraon has strengthened. Towards the end she realizes that her past life is now just a part of her memory, an illusion that has no connection with the reality. Finally she accepts the bitter reality and prepares herself to put up with her loss for the sake of her daughter, Munni.

Syed Muhammad Ashraf (b. 1957) is among the generation of writers who had started writing after Partition. He has published two collections of short stories. One of his short stories 'Man' is the recipient of the Katha Award for Creative Writing. The story 'Separated From the Flock' is translated into English by Vishwamitra Adil and Alok Bhalla from Urdu and is taken from his collection *Dar se Bichre*. In "Separated from the Flock", Syed Muhammad Ashraf also speaks about the anguish of women. Traditionally birds are a symbol of freedom but here they stand for innocence and of women as victims. In the story birds appear as the victims of the cruelty of human beings. They are shot dead and can no longer go back: "O Birds, your wings have been broken. Now you cannot return to those fields of snow!"[25] At this point the writer notes a similarity between the fate of birds and of Ghulam Ali's wife. The birds are shot by guns hence they have got separated from their flock. Their eyes are full of dreams, with visions of "an infinite number of blue and yellow and green birds singing and playing in sheer light amongst giant pine trees covered with snow ... a vision of exultation and joy."[26] Women characters in the story suffer from a sense of alienation and frustration like birds that have been separated from their flock for ever. But the narrator feels that in comparison birds are more fortunate in that they would not have to undergo the pangs of separation for long. On the other hand, these women are in a desperate and worse situation because there is no way out for them and they have to live with this burden throughout their life. Ashraf brings into relief this touching situation: "… our torment never dies, we die slowly, we are hunted without mercy and we can only beat our wings in the throes of death, but cannot die."[27]

Ghulam Ali, the driver, does not want to send his wife on a visit to India. She makes an appeal to let her see and feel, at least once in life, the place of her birth, the place where her identity began. But Ghulam Ali considered her emotional attachment as a whim. He tells the narrator: "I am not concerned about the permit, Sahib. It's not the only problem a man faces in his life, Sahib ……. It's merely a whim – the visit to India. To satisfy that whim, I'll have to waste four to five hundred rupees."[28] Perhaps Ashraf wants to emphasize that one who has not gone through such an experience can never understand the pains of displacement. When a tree is uprooted from its place and planted in an alien land, it gets shrivelled. Same is the case with Jameela. Ghulam Ali's wife. Although she has adopted the life style of a typical Punjabi woman, her mind is not at peace because her roots lie somewhere else. One part of her being constantly pulls her to return to her homeland. The theme of dislocation of women is well-treated by Ashraf.

Aziz Ahmad(1913-1978) is the author of the story *Kali Raat*. The inhumanity with which women were treated during Partition is horrifying. In 'Kali Raat' Abida, one of the women characters, commits suicide when her house is surrounded by rioters. She prefers a dignified death to a condemned life. Thus Abida's act of suicide brings into light the narrow-mindedness of society which imposes taboos of chastity and purity on women only. During Partition when women were abducted and defiled, their society discarded them as if it was their own fault. Such a humiliation provoked many victimized women to commit suicide. Hence Ahmad also raises the issue of women's honour. His stories are not didactic in the strict sense yet they impart lessons to humanity.

Kamleshwar(b. 1932) was closely associated with the 'Nai Kahani' movement in Hindi literature. He has published ten novels, ten short story collections and a number of film scripts. He was also the editor of *Sarika* and *Nai Kahaniyan*, monthly magazines. Kamleshwar's 'How Many Pakistans?' (Kitne Pakistan) was originally written in Hindi and translated into English by K.S.Duggal and included in *Orphans of the Storm: Stories on the Partition of India (1995)*. In 'How Many Pakistans?' The background theme is the relationship between a Muslim girl and a Hindu boy. It is no doubt true that Kamleshwar takes us directly to the deeper consciousness of the narrator, laying bare his soul. But the final picture of a Muslim woman's character which emerges through all this description is dismal and worthy of contempt. Bano is shown as an unfortunate girl who fails to rise to the occasion and finally falls into the life of shame and humiliation. She becomes a prostitute. More significantly, it reflects the mind-set of the writer. Kamleshwar describes the shameful life of Bano with such considerable details as if he is drawing pleasure out of its description. He further justifies this act of Bano by calling it her own way of taking revenge on society as well as her lover.

Muneer, the husband of Bano, is represented as a weak man who fails to support his family. Yet he tries to keep Bano under his control and oppression. Mangal feels helpless when he sees Muneer beating his wife cruelly: "It was terrible to hear you curse and weep, Bano! Each one of us was in agony, each one of us had made our own Pakistan. We had all been disfigured. Mutilated. Crippled. We were only half-alive!"[29] Muneer appears as an intolerant, barbaric and uncivilized person. In contrast, the Hindu characters are presented in a much more favourable light.

Mangal is a helpless victim of Partition. He gets deeply hurt when he sees his beloved in a tragic condition, leading life as a prostitute: "There was a moment of agonizing silence. You, too, had recognized me. There was a venomous smile on your lips or did I imagine it?"[30] Bano is not forced into prostitution. On the contrary, she herself opts the path of filth in order to take revenge which indirectly betrays her weak and fragile character. It is a prejudice that Seraglio (*heram*) is associated often by westerners with Muslim women. In India non-Muslim writers have also followed the Western misperception and have further supported in promoting this tainted picture of Muslim women. The characters of Mumtaz in Malgonkar's *Bend in the Ganges* and of Bano in Kamleshwar's 'How many Pakistans?' confirm this.

In a fit of rage Bano cries out:

> If the maulvis and his followers continue to harass me, I'll eat the dhatura leaves and commit suicide. Don't you dare to leave the town without me. If you do, remember that Gangaji flows nearby. So, think before you ...[31]

The above highlights the agony of a Muslim woman who is deeply in love with a Hindu boy. According to her, it is the cruelty of the orthodox 'Maulvis' which has deprived her of the real happiness of life. It is one of the favourite themes of some non-Muslim writers to condemn Muslims for the strict observance of their faith and they are blamed for making the lives of their innocent womenfolk miserable. Bano's character is also drawn in the same negative light by Kamleshwar. Bano is projected as a poor victim of Partition days who loses everything, especially due to the cruel laws imposed upon her by her own society. However, no one can deny the basic reality that a wrong deed can never be justified. Bano's step to take revenge by committing adultery does not prove her innocence. Rather, it shows that she is a person of weak character.

Numerous Partition stories have dealt with the issues of abduction and rape. Such writings often reflect the trauma of those who have been till this day suffering from a deep feeling of shame and guilt for what their countryman had once done. Khwaja Ahmad Abbas's 'Revenge' too makes alive the horrors of Partition. In this story Hari, the father of a girl who was raped in front of his own eyes, wanders in search of a Muslim girl so that he could kill her and thereby take revenge from the Muslim community as a whole. At last when he succeeds in finding such a girl

"Muslim girl ! Pakistani hoor!!", he raises his dagger to kill her : "Hari Das recognized more than terror in the look – there was fear and hate and a plea for mercy and complete hopelessness. It was the exact look that he had seen in his Janki's eyes". It is tragic that the tragedy of his own daughter turns him from a loving father into a heartless murderer. However all his feelings of hatred for a Muslim girl soften down after he watches the horrible scars on her body telling explicitly the tale of her merciless sexual violation and then "one single word escaped his lips: 'daughter'!". Through this story Abbas seems to give message that the concern for humanity should be the prime motive of all. Whether the victimized woman is a Hindu or a Muslim is not much important, what is significant is her womanhood which should be protected at any cost.

Notes and References

1. Jamila Hashmi, "Banished", trans. from Urdu by M.U. Memon in *An Epic Unwritten* (New Delhi: Penguin, 1998) pp. 87-106.

2. Syed Muhammad Ashraf, "Separated from the Flock", trans. from Urdu by Alok Bhalla in *Stories About the Partition of India*, Vol. I, Delhi: Indus/Herper Collins, 1994, pp. 1-24.

3. Kamleshwar, "How Many Pakistans?", trans. from Hindi by Alok Bhalla in *Stories About the Partition of INdia*, Vol. II, Delhi: Indus/Harper Collins, 1994, pp. 173-190.

4. Rajinder Singh Bedi's "Lajwanti", trans. from the Urdu by M.U. Memon in *An Epic Unwritten* (New Delhi: Penguin, 1998) pp. 87-106.

5. Saadat Hasan Manto, "Mozel", trans. from Urdu by Alok Bhalla in *Stories About the Partition of INdia*, Vol. I, Delhi: Indus/Herper Collins, 1994, pp. 153-172.

6. Ahmad Ali, "Kali Raat", Saros Cowasjee and K.S. Duggal (eds.) *Orphans of the Storm: Stories About the Parttion of India*, New Delhi, UBS Publishers and Distributors, 1995.

7. Mohammad Umar Memon (ed.) *An Epic Unwritten: The Penguin Book of Partition Stories from Urdu*, New Delhi: Penguin Books, 1998, p.95

8. Ibid., p. 87

9. S. Settar and Indira Baptista Gupta (eds.), *Pangs of Partition; the Human Dimension*, Vo.2, New Delhi: Manohar Publishers and Distributors, 2002, p.326.

10. *An Epic Unwritten: The Penguin Book of Partition Stories from Urdu*, p.88.

11. Ibid., p. 90

12. Ibid., p. 91

13. Ibid., p. 104

4. Ibid., p. 88
5. Ibid., p. 93
6. Ibid., p. 92
7. Ibid., p. 101
8. Ibid., p. 91
9. Ibid., p. 102
20. Ibid., p. 99
21. Ibid., pp. 97-98
22. Ibid., p. 102
23. Ibid., p. 101
24. Ravikant and Tarun K. Saint (eds.), *Translating Partition*, New Delhi: Katha, 2001, p. 198.
25. Alok Bhalla (ed.), *Stories about the Partition of India*, Delhi: Indus/Harper Collins, 1994, Vol. 1, p.17.
26. Ibid., p. 14.
27. Ibid., p. 22
28. Ibid., p. 4
29. *Stories about the Partition of India*, Vol. 1, p. 187.
30. Ibid., p. 190
31. Ibid., p. 126

Chapter - 10

Images of Muslim Women in Indian Television Serials

Sabina Kidwai

Serials/Soap operas unlike hard news have been characterized as a feminine genre targeting female audiences. The claim that media output under-represents women has never been applied to this genre, which has been considered as "cinematography expressions of melodrama or as the "women's weepies"' (Byars, 1991). Moreover, with the growth of satellite television, it seems that television is becoming more and more 'feminized' with the growing popularity of soap operas on various channels.

In the fictional format, the soap plays a major role in formulating stereotypes. It is also, however, the most complex form, as it provides spaces to subvert the accepted text. Subversive characters often find space in soaps, which have no place in factual news. Prejudice is an important aspect in soaps but it is a form that also has the potential to subvert prejudice and question it.

As a fictional television form, soaps have distinct characteristics that attract the audiences. Brown (1987) lists eight generic characteristics of soap operas:[1]

1. A serial form that resists narrative closure

2. Multiple characters and plots

3. A use of time that parallels actual time and implies that the action continues to take place whether we watch it or not

4. Abrupt segmentation between parts

5. An emphasis on dialogue, problem solving, and intimate conversation.

6. Male characters who are "sensitive men".

7. Female characters dominate the events of the soaps and vary from housewives to professionals. But situations of emotional entanglements are pre-dominant. The home, or some other place which functions as a home, is the setting for the show.

Traditional realist narratives are constructed to have a beginning, middle, and an end, but soap opera realism works through an infinitely extended middle. Traditional narrative begins with a state of equilibrium that comes to be disturbed, and the plot traces the effects of this disturbance through a middle to find an end that restores equilibrium,. Soaps are never in a state of equilibrium, their world is one of perpetual disturbance and threat. The equilibrium of a happy, stable family is consistently there in the background, but it is never achieved.

In soaps conventional objects – like telephones, doorbell, and surgical mask – have a definite significance, helping or hindering the soap characters' quest. Death is no barrier in soap operas and it is possible to mislay a character, or to have a character reappear from the dead. Soaps are built around ambiguities. One hardly knows who is alive or dead, who is an imposter or the genuine character and kinship relations can be constructed at will.

Soap dialogue is intensely personal, an expression of the deepest emotional conflicts. The most common moment in soap conversation involves two people, one with a personal emotional problem that must be stated and the other with an intense desire to hear the problem. Unhappiness does not really require necessary causes – the characters of soap land are unhappy from the beginning. They have been or are insufficiently loved; perhaps they have been emotionally wounded in the past. The first rule of soaps is that one should not suffer in silence. There may be secrets suppressed in order to advance the plot, but no one ever hides the sources of his or her own discontent. They are all talked out. This is pretty much the opposite of real life, which may constitute one of the principal attractions of the soap opera. Few of us ever get to let the world know exactly how we feel.

Every character has a friend who listens to his or her story. A social illusion is necessarily created that no one is solitary. In the world of soaps, not illusion is necessarily created that no one is solitary. In the world of soaps, not only do we express our deepest feelings, but also the social world listens and responds to them. We are visible in the world of soap opera, far more visible than in reality. And the most visible thing about us is our psychology.

The soap opera is about husbands and wives, its central institution is the family. One of the basic soap plots is about the formation of a family, from the first attraction between two individuals to the social resonance caused by their eventual connection. A soap opera marriage, (and marriages are an important ritual) is not the same as a marriage in a traditional romance in which the couple is expected to live happily ever after. All soap opera marriages have within them the seeds of their own destruction.

One of the big values on soap opera is money. The "bad" characters are corrupt in pursuit of it, but the money itself is legitimate. In fact, the "good" characters' pursuit of it is innocent. There is a kind of pornography of wealth on soap opera, the audience is constantly exposed to designer clothes, jewels, and luxurious homes. The women of soap are not undressed, but overdressed. Here is a make-believe society devoid of politico-economic oppression, inhabited mostly by the rich and affluent middle class, professionals (lawyers, doctors, architects, and business executives and their families) who spend their life wrestling with a never-ending succession of personal crises. Soap characters are not of the working class – in fact there are no class differences and certainly no class conflict. All behavior is seen as morally motivated.

The current soaps appear to be in touch with the times, as they frequently deal with the liberation of women. Societal trends indicate that the membership of women in the work force is growing – the soap responds by miming career women in otherwise domestic settings. Statistics indicate that many real women have risen in the management hierarchy, soaps shows women as high powered executives. However, for every social action there is bound to be a reaction, and not everyone in the audience is liberated. So the soaps keep men in positions of authority. Mothers continue to be best sources of love, sympathy, and advice. Conservative, nurturing women tended to be good characters, while evil women are career – oriented and non-traditional in their behavior.

> Soaps have two sets of characters, the simple and the complex, who tell us not about the news but about ourselves. The simple who are often victims of the complex represent in their innocent way all the hopes and desires of their audience. They want happiness and in order to get it they construct the social, political, and psychological world as if it existed only to respond to human desires. These characters worry us even when they are blameless. The complex characters are, paradoxically, more comfortable to understand. They hover on the edge of drama because they demand real "interaction." And in their powerful self-awareness and emotional selfishness they too help delineate the portrait of an age. Both kinds of characters unite to show recognition of individualism concerned not with political freedom but with emotional indulgence. Thus, without ever actually challenging existing social arrangements, the soaps can come away seeming very relevant by touching upon subjects such as gender roles, rape, incest, spouse abuse, homosexuality, and AIDS. But, again, these things are usually presented as personnel problems to be tackled by personal means.[2]

As Deborah Rogers has observed, soaps are essentially designed within, and in the service of an established patriarchal structure:

> The cumulative effect of introducing in a fragmented text messages that reconcile women to traditional feminine roles and relationships is to reinforce patriarchal cultural behavior in a way that is difficult to identify during a typical that it,

> casual viewing experience … if soaps are featuring more career women, their romances and families take precedence over jobs, which may simply provide sites for gossip and personal relationships. Women who devote too much time to jobs at the expense of their relationships and families are usually punished. Male dominance is ideologically reinforced by the belief that women are gloriously suited for childcare because they are by nature cheerfully domestic, nurturing and self-sacrificing. This "innate" selflessness, essential to fulfilling their roles as wives and mothers, allows for the happiness of women to reside in being constantly attentive to the needs of other family members. Unsurprisingly, on the soaps men give more orders and advice than women.[3]

But the whole genre of soaps is more than a portrayal of the patriarchal ideology. By interrogating the state of marriage it opens up the institution to readings other than those preferred by patriarchy. This double evaluation is generic to soap opera and is part of the reason for its openness. A wife's extra-marital sexual relationship, for instance, is evaluated both patriarchally as unfaithfulness, but also, more interestingly, as a women's independence and right to her own sexuality. As Stuart Hall reports, a study of soap opera fans found that

> women openly and enthusiastically admitted their delight in following soap operas as stories of female transgressions which destroy the ideological nucleus of the text: the priority and sacredness of the family… The dominant ideology is inscribed in the status quo and soap operas offer their subordinated women viewers the pleasure of seeing this status quo in a constant state of disruption. Disruption without resolution produces openness in the text. It can be read dominantly i.e. in patriarchal mould or subversively as the audience decides: such readings would produce fans who return to their more "normal" marriages with a sense of relief.

Soaps also appear to place women characters in positions of power, especially within the domestic sphere. They seem to be more in control of situations than their male counterparts.

> This concern to clarify relationships within the disrupted and unstable family may be seen as "women's matters." That is, as a domain where patriarchy grants women a position of some power. The ability to understand, facilitate, and control relationships is often shown as a source of women's power, used disruptively by the evil women and more constructively by the matriarchs. Men are often shown as deficient in these abilities and knowledge, and cause many problems by this masculine lack. This set of abilities and knowledge, normally devalued by patriarchy, is given a high valuation and legitimating in soap operas, and can serve as a source of self-esteem for the fans as an assertion of women's values against the place assigned to them in patriarchy.[4]

However, one important point stands that in spite of display of women power, the overall text of most soaps works within the norms of patriarchy. So often we find that when the text is closed then subversive display of women power by soap characters gets limited to individual rebellions.

If we look at soaps on Indian prime-time television we find that they are primarily family oriented, and patriarchal in structure. The story is about women characters and good and evil is clearly defined. Women are pivotal to the story their actions move the plots. Men though incidental to everyday events, are integral to the identity of women, the family and soap society. Indian soaps are extremely ritualistic at one level, asserting the ideal religious Hindu joint family as well as a distinct Muslim identity. Traditions, customs, social norms dominate the lives of women. Subversive characters appear, only to be resolved by the ultimate assimilation into the family. Divorce, rape, and marital discord, are addressed but as individual problems. Thus without challenging existing social arrangements, Indian soaps convey a relevance to personal problem to be tackled by personal means.

One fact is uniform, soaps of today are about the rich, wealthy families, where financial problems are only business failures – they are middle class and upper middle class. Soaps in today's globalized society play the integral role of reinforcing Indianness, a return to tradition and the large joint family, wherein the family is both benefactor and friend, and its preservation the mission. They portray a rejection of western influences usually symbolized by the modern woman who disrupts the joint family and she is alienated from Indian traditions and values. The good woman is always the one who lives within the confines of the family and protects it from these external forces of modernity and disruption. At the same time within this outward facade of traditions modernity is ever present-in the form of educated career women and women as decision makers. It is this mix which makes the serial palatable to the middle and upper class audience, as rituals are sold with fun and frolic.

In this make-believe world where does the Muslim woman stand? Is she modern or traditional, assertive or marginalized? Is she still the docile veiled woman of Mere Mehboob or Arzoo? Has she acquired any new identity with the forces of globalization? Is she finally portrayed as a woman with feelings, emotions rather than a victim trapped in religious norms? A review of all prominent soaps, or Muslim socials as they are popularly called, gives us a diverse picture that is mixed in its import, in which change is evident, even though it is marginal.

Henna

The soap Henna on Sony Entertainment Channel is a prime-time serial and received very high ratings in its initial run. I was first introduced to this serial by a friend who described it as a perfect Muslim serial that shows the problems in the Muslim community. She further proceeded to tell me that the story is about a young Muslim woman. Her husband is in love with another woman and periodically threatens to divorce his wife, but the wife stays on and refuses to accept this decision. My friend thought it was a genuine fight of a woman for her rights, against a community of Muslim men who were empowered to threaten their wife in this fashion. Inspired by this rousing summary, I proceeded to watch the serial.

Henna is the story of a young Muslim woman belonging to an affluent business family. She is married into another business family but finds that her husband, Sameer does not care for her. His family has forced him to marry her but he is in love with another woman, Ruby. Henna is a beautiful, fragile looking woman who is liked by all members of her own family as well as her in-laws. She accepts docilely Sameer's rejection and does not tell her in-laws about it. She silently bears his insults, his threats of saying "talaq". She keeps up the pretence of marriage and allows Sameer to continue his affair with Ruby.

Ruby, in contrast, is an outgoing, working woman, who is in love with Sameer and wants him to divorce Henna and marry her. Ruby is vivacious and attractive, but also selfish and mercenary, in perfect contrast to Henna, thereby emphasizing the goodness of the former and the evilness of the latter. In order to reinforce the victim image of Henna, the serial converts Ruby into a self-seeking, avaricious, single working-woman, who is destroying the life of a shy helpless woman. In fact, the attention is directed so much towards this contrast that for some time, the male protagonist, Sameer is rendered exempt from any judgment about his weakness and duplicity in marrying Henna under pressure, despite being in love with Ruby. The war is between the two women, and Sameer returns to the center stage only when the storyteller seems not to be able to find a solution to the problem. This solution is as expected: Sameer reinforces the popular stereotype of Muslim system of divorce when he finally decides that he cannot do without Ruby. In a typical dramatic style he utters the word *talaq* twice and stops. For Henna the marriage is over. She is shattered and goes away to her parents' house as her husband is now a stranger to her.

The next few episodes debate the fact that since Sameer did not say the third *talaq* it may be possible to bring Sameer and Henna back together, as the divorce is incomplete, Henna can be married to Sameer again without *hillala*. *Hillala* is a custom by which if a woman has been divorced, she cannot be married to the same man again. She has to first marry another man, and if he divorces her she can get married to her previous husband. The elders in the family get together and convince Sameer to marry Henna again. Although the elders in the family condemn Sameer's actions, they are not ready to accept the fact that he is in love with somebody else. Henna, too, agrees, to marry Sameer again, despite knowing that he is in love with another woman, and had already once divorced her earlier. Finally the marriage is arranged, but at the ceremony, Sameer pronounces three *talaqs* in front of the gathered guests and finally divorces Henna.

The most disappointing aspect of the serial is that in its attempts to show the unfairness of Muslim Personal Law, it strips women of all respect and even the right of protest. Henna is a pawn in this game of marriage and divorce with no will of her own. She is a mute voiceless victim, who may not be physically veiled but is veiled in her mind and soul. Although she belongs to a supportive modern, rich family and has no financial problems, she cannot even assert her basic rights. Henna's character also appears in contrast with her own sister-in-law Namira, who in the face of marital problems, returns to live with her parents. Namira is supportive of Henna, but the serial does not transform this contrast into the example of Henna.

The tragedy of Henna's life gets further accentuated in the subsequent episodes when she is condemned as a divorced woman rejected by her husband. Meanwhile Ruby disillusioned with Sameer's indecision, refuses to marry Sameer and finds another person, Adnan, who is rich and very much in love with her. Ruby dumps Sameer and gets engaged to Adnan. Sameer is heartbroken and starts regretting his divorce from Henna. A number of episodes are devoted to Sameer's recriminations about his "talaq" to Henna. Meanwhile, Adnan breaks his engagement to Ruby when he gets to know that she had harmed a young defenceless woman like Henna. Ruby tries to come back to Sameer but then Sameer has realized that he is in love with Henna. In all these twists and turns of the plot, Henna is a silent bystander, who neither speaks, nor expresses her anger or her grief – she just looks tragic.

When changes do happen in Henna's life, she once again has no control over them. She meets Akram, an old friend of Sameer, who had been supportive of Henna during the divorce. Although the serial indicates that she supports and helps Akram in a business venture, we never see her doing any work. (Actually nobody in the serial seems to do any work. They go to office but spend all their time with personal problems.) Finally on her parents' insistence, Henna marries Akram, who is a caring and decent man. But her tragic past will not leave Henna, and she refuses to have marital relations with Akram, and asks for time. Once again she becomes a victim, and this time she is harassed and persecuted by an aunt of Akram, who had wanted Akram to marry her niece. Eventually the niece arrives and disrupts Henna's marital life. On the other hand, Sameer starts cherishing dreams of *Hillala*, and continues to yearn for Henna. Henna starts to care for Akram but fears losing him to the niece. The marital discord is resolved with the death of the niece, but Sameer's passion and hope of *Hillala* continue to loom large over Henna's life.

Thus the intricate drama goes on, with the typical soap logic of the hope of resolution in a life that continues to be in a perpetual state of disturbance. The setting of the serial is modern, all characters dress well, they work in corporate houses, live in luxurious homes, and do not follow any of the Muslim stereotypes in physical appearances. However, their personal lives are in a constant upheaval on the issue of *talaq*, an aspect of Muslim Personal Law which reinforces the lack of agency of Muslim women. Their relationship with religion and God seems to be around this issue and all other problems are immaterial. All characters are Muslim and the whole social world is Muslim.

Henna's tragedy is emphasized in the title song which is about a broken world, a destroyed home, and is accompanied with visuals of Henna in various wedding dresses, tragic and mute questioning her fate (and the audiences) for the vicissitudes that she has to undergo in the modern world.

Shaheen

Shaheen is the story of a young woman living in Mumbai, who is married into a feudal Nawab family in Lucknow, Shaheen wants to study but pressured by her father, she agrees to marry Junaid. After her marriage she discovers that Junaid is a widower, and was once married to Nadira and has a son by her. She is shocked by this reality, and decides to leave Junaid and returns back to Mumbai. Junaid tells her that he had told her parents about his earlier wife and his son Suhail, and is shocked that she was not told about it. He accepts her decision to return back to Mumbai.

On her return to Mumbai, Shaheen finds that her father is ill, and so decided not to inform him of her circumstances. Trapped by events, she asks Junaid to come and take her back, and life transports Shaheen from the urban setting of Mumbai to the feudal life of Lucknow. The family are rich princely Zamindars, living in a large *Haveli* with ornate carvings and a feudal structure of *Mardana/Zanana*[5]. All the order characters in the serial like the mother-in-law, aunts, wear the traditional Muslim dress, *gharara*. Visually, it has all the symbolism of an exotic society, but it reflects also the gradual destruction of a culture, a family trapped between the values of the old and new, a society in flux trying to hold on to a dying culture. This is a society following old traditions, with a resistance to accepting the changing world outside. Into this complex situation is drawn Shaheen. On one side she is the wife of a cultured respected Nawab, the *bahu* of the family, the mother of growing child, on the other she has her own desires, a desire to be free, to study. Shaheen has also to battle with the ghost of Nadira, who seems to dominate the mind of all members of the household. Although Shaheen gradually develops a relationship with her husband, she also discovers his intense passion for his dead wife. Unable to forget Nadira, Junaid seems trapped in his past. And Shaheen becomes a victim of these circumstances.

In spite of its feudal setting, the serial is complex in its portrayal of women characters. The character of Shaheen is constantly evolving. Junaid understands Shaheen's needs and allows Shaheen to pursue her studies. It is here that we see how Shaheen crosses the boundaries of tradition. She moves out everyday from the strictly Zenana household into the Mardana world of the college. She adjusts the needs of both the worlds, juggling them so as to ensure hereself some freedom. It is in College that she interacts with other women of her age and gets involved in flirtations with other fellow students, most prominently a young poet who falls in love with Shaheen (a recreation of the stereotype of the "Shayar"). The intensity of the passion is reminiscent of the idealized poet of Mere Mehboob and Arzoo. The entire college setting has constant reference to Urdu poets like Ghalib and Mir. The students have poetry sessions, and globalization is still an event of the future. This world of the college is far away from Shaheen's *haveli*, more alive and more real, but since the serial focuses on Shaheen and her changes, the contrast between these worlds does not disturb us.

Shaheen, like all the *mehboobas* of *shayars*, remains oblivious of the poet's passion and continues struggle at home with the image of Nadira. The interesting part of the character of Shaheen in that though she is shown as a conventionally Muslim woman, there is no undue emphasis on religion, or personal, law. At one level the Muslim aspect is reinforced in the props used in the sets but it is underplayed on the other level of her individual struggle. Shaheen's relationship with a young lady doctor is also very interesting. Shobha, and independent working-woman, encourages Shaheen to find a place for herself and often tells her to remain Shaheen and not to try and become Nadira, otherwise she would lose her individual identity. Shaheen provides support to Shobha, when the latter faces marital discord about their childlessness. Shobha decides to undergo a fertility test and is cleared, but her husband refuses to take it, and accuses Shobha of doubting his manhood. Shobha's marriage is on the brink of divorce. Shobha finds empathy in Shaheen. The sensitivity of the serial is that it never shows its women characters as weak, rather foregrounds how circumstances/events control people's lives and how they negotiate to find spaces within it.

The contrast to Shaheen's character is provided by the images of Nadira. She is described as a headstrong, aggressive, vivacious woman. But through the serial a strange bond develops between the two characters. Shaheen's initial hostility to Nadira changes as she realizes the same feelings of being trapped. Eventually Shaheen unable to take Junaid's indifference leaves and goes back to her parents. Here a struggle begins in her search for a new identity.

The serial has some other interesting characters – the mother-in-law, and Shaheen's own mother. The mother-in-law though feudal in her outlook, gives considerable support to Shaheen. Shaheen's mother is shown as having been kept in the dark about the fact that her daughter was to be married to a widower with a child. When she realizes this, she does not forgive Shaheen's father, and asks Shaheen to return if she is not happy. She actively encourages her son to defy father and marry a woman of his own choice.

Another interesting character is Ghuncha, Shaheen's sister-in-law, who is stuck in an unhappy marriage. It is her life which clearly reflects the decaying trends of an old society. Her husband Zulfiqar is a Nawab whose family has lost all their wealth. He lives on the monthly cheque sent by Junaid and takes out all his frustrations on Ghuncha. He dreams of a glorious tomorrow, but spends his present criticizing the world for his problems. At some point Ghuncha leaves him but finally returns to keep the marriage going. Her anger, frustrations all find reflection in the serial and she is not a silent victim.

The title song of soap is also sung in the old style, but it does talk of hope, a brighter future and a woman's desire to live. The setting is exotic, Oriental and beautiful, in fact the title music sets the serial in another time period, whereas the events are very much in the present. The sense of time is ambiguous in the serial. However, the popularity of the serial has waned as it has lost its prime-time slot of Wednesday and has been shifted to Friday morning.

Tanha

Tanha on Star Plus is the story of a rich Muslim family, urban and educated. The head of the household is Shakeela Begum, who is an independent working woman. She runs a business and the house/ sets suggest affluence and considerable wealth. It is apparent that the serial was attempting to follow the style of popular Pakistani plays. These plays are centered around a family and the emotional involvement of its members. Heseena Moeen, the writer of Tanha, is also the writer of many Pakistani plays like Dhop Kinara, Ankahi, etc. The language of the play, though

Urdu, simple and attractive, but the soap lacks much of the humour and punch of Pakistani plays.

The characters of Tanha seem to be set in an alien setting, isolated from the world outside. Shakeela Begum runs a business house but we never see her office or the nature of her business. She goes to office but only seems to be signing papers, with no concrete evidence of work. In fact, both at home and in the office, she bears a tragic air. She is a widow. However, the tragedy is not the death of her husband but some mysterious event in the past. She has two sons and two daughters, they are also independent and working.

The elder daughter Ruksana is married and is initially shown as happily married. Gradually her marital bliss is destroyed by her discovery that her husband is having an affair with another woman. She continues to be torn by tragedy and does not tell her mother. After many years of marriage she discovers she is pregnant but loses the child in a car accident. He husband serves her divorce papers, and unable to take this final humiliation, she commits suicide.

In spite of being a serial with predominantly Muslim characters, the issue of *talaq* is not raised, not of second marriage, and divorce papers are served with limited dramatic intensity. It is quite evident that the serial does attempt to underplay the Muslim identity of its characters in their daily living. They go through their trials and tribulations without being traumatized by religious norms. Although the tragedy of Shakeela Begum's past involves an earlier marriage, it has none of the religious connotations. She was married to a Nawab, who is one of his drunken stupor drinks poison. Scared of being accused of killing him, Shakeela runs away with the help of a friend leaving her child behind. The friend fails to contact her later and she is cut off from meeting her child, even after the case is resolved. This child from the past appears and wants Shakeela Begum to accept him. The story depicts the emotional struggle of Shakeela Begum in wanting to accept her child, and the fear of the effect it many have on her children and present life. Another character is introduced in the role of,a niece from London (played by a well known Pakistani actress), who is supposed to be lively and unconventional; however, she leaves in the middle of the serial.

The problem in the soap is that it never developed any roots, the story remained disjointed, the sets were alien, the society too isolated from the real world, a world of the Muslim elite in India just did not fit in the Indian cultural setting. The serial attempts to create the ambience of Pakistani plays but is not able to evolve the characters. In fact the real problem is that the characters and their lives seem to be static in time.

The title Tanha and the title song both suggest loneliness and alienation. Shakeela Begum is lonely in spite of being with her family. Her lost child is also a lonely, alienated individual. The serial does try and raise the loneliness every individual feels in their alien world.

Jannat

Jannat is a soap opera telecast on metro channel, Doordarshan in the prime-time slot of 9:00 to 10:00 pm on Friday and Saturday. It is the story of a Muslim family with one daughter Naz and a niece Jannat. Naz is happily married to a sensible man Adnan and is treated well by her in-laws. Jannat is engaged to be married to Kabir, and the whole household is full of activity around the impending marriage. The visual image of Jannat is of a pretty vivacious young woman, who is loved by everybody. She has been brought up by her uncle and aunt who consider her their daughter. She is protected, innocent and unaware of the problems of the world. She is very attached to her cousin sister Naz.

Jannat's world is disrupted when she realizes that her sister is facing marital problems. Adnan and Naz, though happily married, cannot have a child because Naz is infertile. Adnan's family, though they care for Naz, want a child and the mother-in-law constantly talks about the lack of a *waris* (heir). The issue takes a serious turn when Adnan's parents decide to get him married again for the sake of a child, although they simultaneously emphasize that they do not want to deny Naz her rights or demote her in status. Adnan refuses and is loyal to Naz, but it is Naz, the perpetual victim, who insists that he should get married again. She takes on the mantle of protecting the interests of the family, and prepares to sacrifice her own for the greater good.

Polygamy for the sake of a child is thus justified and reinforced in the soap, and therefore legitimizes the right of polygamy of Muslim men. On the other hand, it negates divorce as something unacceptable and un-Islamic. In one episode, Naz says, "I prefer to allow Adnan to marry again rather than allow *talaq* to be added to my name". This anti-divorce position is also emphasized in the character of Noora, a divorcee. Noora is shown as a hard-headed nasty woman, who desperately wants to marry Adnan, but also wants to break up the family. She is described as an evil woman, "otherwise, why would she be divorced?" In fact, in one episode, Kabir's parents tell Jannat's parents that though they feel that Adnan should get married again, for Naz's sake, it should not be to the divorcee, Noora.

So polygamy is justified but not divorce. The issue is centered around Naz's ability to have a child, emphasizing the woman's role as the procreator, with polygamy being justified if the woman fails to perform this essential role. The fact that Adnan does not want to marry is immaterial and when he refuses, Naz threatens divorce (*Khula*) which is unacceptable to Adnan also. Jannat and Kabir tragically sacrifice their happiness so that Jannat can eventually get married to Adnan. Both suffer – Kabir is socially ostracized for refusing to marry Jannat, saying that she is barren and Jannat for being rejected. So events lead up to Adnan marrying Jannat with Naz's consent. A key role is also played by Zoya, Adnan's sister, who wants to marry Aamir, Noora's brother. Zoya is also portrayed as a selfish woman who is ready to sacrifice the happiness of her good *bhabi* for her own interest. The fact women are women's own enemies is constantly emphasized.

The serial, instead of giving women some dignity, strips them of any individuality or identity. All the women characters in the serial are educated, affluent, well dressed but do not work, all their time is spent on emotional crisis and around religious events.

The serial further addresses the issue of *talaq*, a favourite of all Muslim soaps on television. Conflict emerges between the two sisters and Naz starts resenting Jannat's involvement with Adnan. Naz, who is not aware that Jannat had married Adnan to ensure a secure life for Naz, starts doubting Jannat's intentions and feels that she is being displaced from her position. Petty jealousies take a wrong turn when Naz accuses Jannat of being pregnant with Kabir's child. She claims that Jannat has been meeting Kabir secretly and is pregnant and produces a report to prove her point. Jannat claims that she is not pregnant and goes for another test. Adnan shocked by Naz's accusation, threatens to divorce her if Jannat's report is negative. As expected the report is negative, but in order to save her sister, Jannat says that the report is positive. She asks Adnan to give her *khula* for her misdeeds. In a practice unheard of in Islam, the serial shows Adnan declaring divorce three times – "Main ne tumko *khula* diya" – a unique subversion of the rights of women to divorce under Islam. The announcement is made publicly, giving a legitimacy to the whole act of verbal instantaneous divorce. Jannat, now a divorcee and therefore, an immoral woman, leaves the house and is ostracized by her family and also by society.

The story of Jannat revolves around the issue of polygamy and the serial goes to a large extent in explaining the circumstances in which polygamy is valid. The plot of the serial is quite bizarre, with a wide social religious acceptability being given to a second marriage, the emerging conflict between the two sisters and the submissive role of a husband who claims to love his wife very much. The practice of instantaneous, verbal talaq is highlighted thus enforcing all the stereotypes of a Muslim family. The character of Jannat is an example of the submissive, self-sacrificing Muslim woman oppressed by her family. Religious practices are limited to marriage and divorce, in an otherwise, modern urban setting. The placing of the women in the context of marriage is predominant in the serial.

Other Serials

There are a few other serials that deal with Muslim families, such as Adhikar, Amma and Family, Rehnuma. Adhikar was initially telecast on Zee TV in the 9.00 pm slot during 1999, and re-telecast in the afternoon slot during 2000. The story is based on a feudal family in Hyderabad. A Nawab divorces his earlier wife and marries a young woman Shama Begum and has a child by her. The Nawab dies and since the divorce was not through a written document, the earlier wife claims that she was not divorced and is entitled to the property. Shama Begum does not have a written *Nikahnama* and the Qazi defaults as a witness, allowing the lawyers to accuse her of being the Nawab's mistress. Shama Begum loses the case and is devoid of all the property of her husband. The serial deals with the story of Shama Begum and her fight for recognition and right to property. It is also the story of the young lawyer who is plagued by guilt with the way in which he deprived Shama Begum of her rights. The difference between this serials and the others is that at least here the protagonist makes an attempt to fight for her rights. The setting is a feudal Hyderabadi family but the evolution of Shama's character is progressive.

Another engaging serial was Amma and Family, which was also telecast in 1999. The serial revolves around a middle-class Muslim family that is urban and modern. It is culturally Muslim but there was no excessive religiosity or marital discords. Amma, the central character is a progressive old woman, whose various crises in life add the comic element to the serial. This was one serial that was able to portray an average educated Muslim family were the women had all the rights and were modern in their thinking. However, both Adhikar and Amma and Family never enjoyed the same success as Henna and Jannat. The channels also did not feel the need to give these serials better time slots.

In conclusion, it is evident that the ideal portrayal of a Muslim woman continues to be a docile, submissive character who is burdened by family pressures and religious sanctions. She is fragile, beautiful, but has no voice or agency. She is a victim of religious marriage and divorce laws. Even in a modern setting, women are never able to escape their religious identity. However, there are spaces even in this negative picture. The Muslim women characters are educated, they are not *burqa*-clad and do sometimes have a better survival instinct as in the case of Shaheen. Spaces also exist in the portrayal of supportive characters as the characters of Namira in Henna and the character of Zoya in Jannat.

Notes and References

1. Stuart Hall, "The Whites of Their Eyes: Racist Ideologies and the Media" in *Gender, Race and Class*, edited by Gail Dines and Jean M. Humez, Sage Publications, 1995.

2. "Sops, Day and Night, How television sees its Audiences."

3. Deborah Rogers, "Daze of our lives, The Soap Opera as a Feminine Text" in *Gender, Race and Class*, edited by Gail Dines and Jean M. Humez, Sage Publications, 1995.

4. Stuart Hall, *Op. Cit.*

5. *Mardana, Zanana* – In feudal society the houses are divided into the outside world of men (*mardana*) and the inner protected world of *Zanana* (women). This also enforced the *purdah* system in traditional societies.

Bibliography

Compiled by
Md. Mahmudul Hasan
University of Portsmouth, UK

Abu-Lughod, Lila. *Veiled Sentiments: Honor and Poetry in a Bedouin Society*. California: University of California Press, 2000.

——. "Do Muslim Women Really Need Saving? Anthropological Reflections on Cultural Relativism and Its Others." *American Anthropologist,* 104:3 (2002): 783–790.

Abu Sulayman, Abdul Hamid. *Marital Discord: Recapturing the Full Islamic Spirit of Human Dignity*. Herndon, VA: International Institute of Islamic Thought, 2003.

Afkhami, Mahnaz (ed.). *Faith and Freedom: Women's Human Rights in the Muslim World*. London: Tauris, 1995.

——. "Claiming Our Rights: A Manual for Women's Human Rights Education in Muslim Societies." In *Muslim Women and the Politics of Participation: Implementing the Beijing Platform*, ed. Mahnaz Afkhami, & Erika Friedl. Syracuse: Syracuse University Press, 1997, 109–120.

——. "Promoting Women's Rights in the Muslim World." *Journal of Democracy*, 8:1 (1997), 157–167.

——, & Haleh Vaziri. *Claiming Our Rights: A Manual for Women's Human Rights Education in Muslim Societies*. Bethesda, MD: Sisterhood is Global, 1996.

Aftab, Tahira. "Reform Societies and Women's education in Northern India in the later 19th century." *Journal of the Pakistan Historical Society*, 35 (April 1987).

Agarwal, Bina (ed.). *Structures of Patriarchy: The State, the Community, and the Household in Modernising Asia*. London: Zed Books, 1988.

Ahmad, Fawzia. "Still 'In Progress?'—Methodological Dilemmas, Tensions and Contradictions in Theorizing South Asian Muslim Women." In *South Asian Women in the Diaspora*, ed. Nirmal Puwar & Parvati Raghuram. New York: Berg, 2003, 43–65.

——. "Engaging a New Discourse: Teaching 'Women in Islam' in the American University Classroom." *Journal of Feminist Studies in Religion*, 18:2 (2002): 131–140.

Ahmad, Khurshid. *Family Life in Islam*. Leicester: The Islamic Foundation, 1974.

Ahmad, Nazir (1869). *Mirat ul-Urus* (Mirror of the Bride), trans. M. Kempson. Hogarth Press, 1934.

——. *Banat un Na'ash* (Daughters), Delhi, 1872.

—— (1874). *The Repentance of Nussooh, Taubat-al-Nasuh: the tale of a Muslim family a hundred years ago*, ed. C. M. Naim, trans. M. Kempson. New Delhi: Permanent Black, 2004.

——. *Mubtala: or, A tale of two wives, an oriental novel, illustrating the different phases of Musalman life in India*, trans. and abridg. Khaja Khan. Madras: Hogarth Press, 1934

Ahmad, Rukhsana (ed. & trans.). *Beyond Belief: Contemporary Feminist Urdu Poetry*. Lahore: ASR Publications, 1990.

Ahmed, Leila. "Western Ethnocentrism and Perceptions of the Harem." *Feminist Studies*, 8:3, (1982): 521-534.

——. *Women and Gender in Islam: Historical Roots of a Modern Debate*. New Haven: Yale University Press, 1992.

——. "Encounter with American Feminism: A Muslim Woman's View of Two Conferences." *Women's Studies Quarterly*, 25:1–2 (1997), 268–270.

Ahmed, Nilufer, Gladis Kaufman, & Shamim Naim. "South Asian Families in the United States: Pakistani, Bangladeshi and Indian Muslims." In *Family and Gender among American Muslims*, ed. Barbara C. Aswad, & Barbara Bilgé. Philadelphia: Temple University Press, 1996, 155–172.

Al-Faruqi, Lamya. *Women, Muslim Society and Islam*. Indianapolis, IN: American Trust Publications, 1991.

Alghamdi, Amani. "Bringing a Global Education Perspective to Understand 'the Other': A Case Study of Western Myths of Muslim Women." Mount Saint Vincent University, Canada, 2002. (MA thesis)

Al-Hibri, Azizah. "An Introduction to Muslim Women's Rights." In *Windows of Faith, Muslim Women Scholar-Activists in North America*, ed. Gisela Webb. New York: Syracuse University Press, 2000, 51–71.

——. "Islam, Law, and Custom: Redefining Muslim Women's Rights." *American University Journal of International Law and Policy*, 12:1 (1997), 1–44.

——. "A Study of Islamic Herstory: Or How Did We Get into This Mess?" *Women's Studies International Forum*, 5 (1982), 207–219.

—— *Women and Islam*. New York: Pergammon Press, 1985.

Ali, Azra Asghar. "Recovery of Female Voice through Women's Journals in Urdu in British India 1898-1947." *South Asia*, 21:1 (1998), 61-86.

——. *The Emergence of Feminism Among Indian Muslim Women 1920-1947*. Karachi: Oxford University Press, 2000.

Ali, Mrs Meer Hasan. *Observations on the Mussulmans of India* (1832). Karachi: Oxford University Press, 1978.

Ali, Mubarak. "*Bahishti Zewar* and the Image of Muslim Women." *South Asia Bulletin*, 8:1-2 (1988), 59-63.

Ali, Sayyed Mumtaz. *Huquq un-Niswan* [Rights of Women]. 1898.

Ali, Shaheen S. *Gender and Human Rights in Islam and International Law: Equal Before Allah, Unequal Before Man?* The Hague: Kluwer Law International, 2000.

Ali, Syed Ameer. *Woman in Islam*. Lahore: The Mohammadan Tract and Book Depot, 1893.

——. "The Influence of Women in Islam." *The Nineteenth Century*, May, 1899.

Alloula, Malek. *The Colonial Harem*. Minneapolis: The University of Minnesota Press, 1986.

Amin, Sonia Nishat. *The World of Muslim Women in Colonial Bengal, 1876-1939*. Leiden, E. J. Brill, 1996.

——. "Rokeya Sakhawat Hossain and the Legacy of the 'Bengal Renaissance." *Journal of the Asiatic Society of Bangladesh*, 34:2 (1989), 185-192.

An-Na'im, Abdullahi A. (ed.) *Islamic Family Law in a Changing World: A Global Resource Book*. New York: Zed Books, 2002.

Anwar, Ghazala. "Muslim Feminist Discourses." In *Feminist Theology in Different Contexts*, ed. Elisabeth S. Fiorenza, & Shawn Copeland. London: SCM Press, 1996, 55–61.

Ashrafi, Talat. A. *Muslim Women in Changing Perspective*. Delhi: Commonwealth Publishers, 1992.

Azim, Firdous, & Niaz Zaman (eds.). *Infinite Variety: Women in Society and Literature*. Dhaka: University Press Limited, 1994.

Badawi, Jamal A. *Gender Equality in Islam: Basic Principles.* Indianapolis, IN: American Trust Publication, 1995.

——. *The Status of Women in Islam*. Plainfield, IN: American Trust Publications, 1995.

Badran, Margot. "Understanding Islam, Islamism, and Islamic Feminism." *Journal of Women's History*, 13:1 (2001), 47–54.

Bald, Suresht R. "Coping with Marginality: South Asian Women Immigrants in Britain." In *Feminism/Postmodernism/Development*, ed. Marianne H. Marchland, & Jane L. Parpat. London: Routledge, 1995, 110–126.

Barr, Pat. *The Memsahibs: In Praise of the Women of Victorian India.* London: Century, 1989.

Behdad, Ali. "The Eroticized Orient: Images of the Harem in Montesquieu and His Precursors." *Stanford French Review*, 13 (1989): 109-126.

Bhalla, Alok. (ed.) *Stories about the Partition of India* (3 Vols). Delhi: Indus/Harper Collins, 1994.

Barlas, Asma. *Believing Women in Islam: Unreading Patriarchal Interpretations of the Quran.* Austin: University of Texas Press, 2002.

Barton, Mukti. "Rokeya Sakhawat Hossain and the Bengali Muslim Women's Movement." *Dialogue and Alliance*, 12:1 (1998), 105-116.

Bewley, Aisha A. *Islam: The Empowering of Women*. London: Ta-Ha, 1999.

Bilgrami, Fatima Z. "Sir Syed's Views on Female Education." *Journal of the Pakistan Historical Society*; 44:3 (1996), 243-257.

Billington, Mary Frances. *Woman in India; by Mary Frances Billington. With an Introduction by the Marchioness of Dufferin and Ava*. London: Chapman and Hall, 1895.

Beck, Lois, & Nikki Keddie (eds.). *Women in the Muslim World*. Cambridge: Harvard University Press, 1978.

Bharucha, Nilufer E. "From behind a Fine Veil: A Feminist Reading of Three Parsi Novels." *Indian Literature*, 39:5 (1996), 132-41.

Blanks, David R., & Michael Frassetto. *Western Views of Islam in the Medieval and Early Modern Europe: Perception of Other*. New York: St. Martin's Press, 1999.

Borthwick, Meredith. *The Changing Role of Women in Bengal 1849-1905*. Princeton: Princeton University Press, 1984.

Bullock, Katherine. "Media (Mis)Representations: Muslim Women in the Canadian Nation." *Canadian Woman Studies/Les Cahiers de la Femme*, 20:2 (2000), 35-40.

——. *Rethinking Muslim Women and the Veil: Challenging Historical & Modern Stereotypes*. Herndon, VA: The International Institute of Islamic Thought, 2002.

Burton, Antoinette. *Dwelling in the Archive: Women Writing House, Home, and History in Late Colonial India*. New York: Oxford University Press, 2003.

——. *Burden of History: British Feminists, Indian Women, and Imperial Culture, 1865-1915*. Chapel Hill: University of North Carolina Press, 1994.

Burton, Isabel. *AEI: Arabia, Egypt, India: A Narrative of Travel*. London, 1879.

Butalia, Urvashi. *The Other Side of Silence: Voices from the Partition of India*. Delhi: Penguin Books, 1998.

Cary, Amelia. *Chow-Chow; Being Selections from a Journal kept in India, Egypt and Syria (*2 vols). London: Hurst and Blackett, 1857.

Chhachhi, Amrita. "The State, Religious Fundamentalism, and Women: Trends in South Asia." *Economic and Political Weekly*, 24:11 (1989)< 567-578.

Chance, Jane. *Woman as Hero in Old English Literature*. Syracuse: Syracuse University Press, 1986.

Chew, Shirley, & Anna Rutherford (ed.). *Unbecoming Daughters of the Empire*. UK: Dangaroo Press, 1993.

Cooke, Miriam. "Multiple Critique: Islamic Feminist Rhetorical Strategies." In *Postcolonialism, Feminism, and Religious Discourse*, ed. Laura. E. Donaldson, & Pui-lan Kwok, London: Routledge, 2002, 142-160.

Cooper, Elizabeth. *The Harim and the Purdah: Studies of Oriental Women*. London: 1915.

Cousins, Margaret. *History of Indian Women's Movement*. Delhi: Stri Dharma, 1935.

Cowasje, Saros, & K. S. S. Duggal (eds.). *Orphans of the Storm: Stories on the Partition of India*. New Delhi, UBS, 1995.

Croutier, Alev Lytle. *Harem: The World Behind the Veil*, ed. Alan Axelrod. New York: Abbeville, 1989.

Darwish, L. "Images of Muslim Women: 'Aisha, Fatima, and Zaynab bint 'Ali in Contemporary Gender Discourse." *McGill Journal of Middle East Studies*, 4 (1996), 93–132.

Das, Gurcharan. *A Fine Family*. Delhi: Penguin Books, 1990.

Dasgupta, Shamita D. "Gender Roles and Cultural Continuity in the Asian Indian Immigrant Community in the US." *Sex Roles*, 38:11–12 (1998), 953–974.

——. *A Patchwork Shawl: Chronicles of South Asian Women in America*. New Brunswick: Rutgers University Press, 1998.

De, Dhurjati Prosad. "Women's Liberation Movement among the Bengal Muslims: A Study of Early 20th Century Social Phenomenon." *Quarterly Review of Historical Studies* [India], 26:4 (1987), 25-32.

Desai, Shashinath K (ed.). *Contemporary Indian Short Stories*. Delhi: Sahitya Akademy, 2003.

De Souza, E. *Purdah: An Anthology*. New Delhi: Oxford University Press, 2004.

Devji, Faisal Fatehali. "Gender and Politics of Space: The Movement for Women's Reform in Muslim India, 1857-1900." *South Asia* [Australia], 14:1 (1991), 141-153.

Donaldson, Laura E. *Decolonizing Feminisms: Race, Gender, and Empire-Building*. London: Routledge, 1993.

Donaldson, Laura E., & Kwok Pui-lan (ed.). *Postcolonialism, Feminism, and Religious Discourse*. New York, London: Routledge, 2002.

Dua, Enakshi. "Racism or Gender: Understanding Oppression of South Asian-Canadian Women." *Canadian Woman Studies*, 13:1 (1992), 6–10.

Dutta, Kalyani. "Rokeya Sakhawat Hosain's *Gyanphal* and *Muktiphal*: A Critique of the Iconography of the Nation-as-Mother." *Indian Journal of Gender Studies*, 7:2 (2000), 203-216.

Dwyer, Claire. "Contested Identities: Challenging Dominant Representations of Young British Muslim Women." In *Cool Places: Geographies of Youth Cultures*, ed. Tracy Skelton, & Gill Valentine. London: Routledge, 1997, 50–65.

——. "Contradictions of Community: Questions of Identity for Young British Muslim Women." *Environment and Planning*, 31

(1999), 53–69.

——. "Negotiating Diasporic Identities: Young British South Asian Muslim Women." *Women's Studies International Forum*, (2000), 475–487.

——. "Veiled Meanings: Young British Muslim Women and the Negotiation of Differences." *Gender Place and Culture: A Journal of Feminist Geography*, 6:1 (1999), 5–27.

Edwards, Holly. *Noble Dreams, Wicked Pleasures: Orientalism in America, 1870-1930*. Princeton: Princeton University Press in association with Sterling Francine and the Clark Art Institute, 2000.

El Guindi, Fadwa. *Veil: Modesty, Privacy, and Resistance*. Oxford: Berg, 1999.

El-Solh, Camillia Fawzi (ed. and introd.). *Muslim Women's Choices: Religious Belief and Social Reality*; Providence, RI: Berg, 1995.

Engineer, Asghar Ali. *Status of Women in Islam*. Delhi: Ajanta Publications, 1987.

——. *The Rights of Women in Islam*. New Delhi: Sterling Publishers, 1992.

Esposito, John. *Women in Muslim Family Law*. Syracuse: Syracuse University Press, 1982.

Fernea, Elizabeth Warnock. *In Search of Islamic Feminism: One Woman's Global Journey*. New York: Doubleday, 1998.

——. "Islamic Feminism Finds a Different Voice: The Muslim women's movement is discovering its roots in Islam, not in imitating Western feminists." *Foreign Service Journal* – 2000. Retrieved October 27, 2004 from http://www.afsa.org/fsj/may00/fernea.cfm

Forbes, Geraldine. "The Indian Women's Movement: A Struggle for Women's Rights or National Liberation?" In *The Extended Family: Women and Political Participation in India and Pakistan*, ed. Gail Minault. Delhi: Chanakya Publications, 1981, 49-82.

——. *Women in Modern India*. Vol. 4, *The Cambridge History of India*. Cambridge: Cambridge University Press, 1996.

Fuller, Marcus B. (ed.). *The Wrongs of Indian Womanhood*. Edinburgh, Oliphant Anderson and Ferrier, 1990.

Futehally, Zeenuth. *Zohra*. New Delhi: Oxford University Press, 2004.

Gargi, Balwant. *Purple Moonlight*. New Delhi, UBSPD, 1994.

Ghosh, Ratna. "South Asian Women in Canada: Adaptation." In *South Asians in the Canadian Mosaic*, ed. R. N. Kanungo, Montreal: Kala Bharati, 1984, 145–155.

Gole, Nilufer. *The Forbidden Modern: Civilization and Veiling*. Ann Arbor: University of Michigan Press, 1996.

Gomis, Annette. "Purdah and Power: Unveiling the Links." *Revista Canaria de Estudios Ingleses*, 45 (2002), 101-19.

Gordon, Haim, Leonard Grob, & Riffat Hassan (eds.). *Women's and Men's Liberation: Testimonies of Spirit*. Westport: Greenwood Press, 1991.

Graham-Brown, Sarah. *Images of Women: The Portrayal of Women in Photography of the Middle East 1860-1950*. New York: Columbia University Press, 1988.

Grewal, Inderpal. *Home and Harem: Nation, Gender, Empire, and the Cultures of Travel*. Durham and London: Duke University Press, 1996.

Gupta, Sangeeta. *Emerging Voices: South Asian American Women: Redefining Self, Family and Community*. Walnut Creek, CA: Alta Mira Publications, 1999.

Haddad, Yvonne Y., & John L. Esposito (ed.). *Daughters of Abraham: Feminist Thought in Judaism, Christianity and Islam*. Gainesville, FL: University Press of Florida, 2001.

Rusva, Mirza Muhammad Hadi . *Amrao Jan Ada*, trans. David Matthews. New Delhi: Rupa, 1996.

Hali, Altaf Husain. *Majalisunissa*, Delhi,1874.

Hallissy, Margaret. *Venomous Woman: Fear of the Female in Literature*. New York: Greenwood, 1987.

Haque, Anees-ul. *Firdaus*. New Delhi: Harman Publishing House, 2003.

Haque, Riffat Ayesha. *Purdah of the Heart and the Eyes: An Examination of Purdah as an Institution in Pakistan*. University of New South Wales, 2004. (dissertation)

Hasan, Md. Mahmudul. "The Orientalization of Gender." *American Journal of Islamic Social Sciences*, 22:4 (2005), 26-56.

Hasan, Mushirul. *India Partitioned: The Other Face of Freedom*, 2 Vols. Delhi: Roli Books, 1995.

——, & Asaduddin, M (ed.) *Image and Representation: Stories of Muslim Lives in India*. New Delhi: Oxford University Press, 2000.

Hasan, Zoya, & Ritu Menon. *Unequal Citizens: A Study of Muslim Women in India*. New Delhi: Oxford University Press, 2004.

Hasanat, Fayaza S. *Recasting Muslim Women: A Translation of Nawab Faizunnesa's 'Rupjalal', with Commentary*. University of Florida, 2005. (PhD thesis)

Hashmi, Taj I. *Women and Islam in Bangladesh: Beyond Subjection and Tyranny*. New York: St Martin's Press, 2000.

Hassan, Riffat. "Challenging the Stereotypes of Fundamentalism: An Islamic Feminist Perspective." *The Muslim World*, 91:1-2 (2001), 55–70.

——. "Equal before Allah? Woman-Man Equality in the Islamic Tradition." *Harvard Divinity Bulletin*, 17:2 (1987), 2–14.

——. "Muslim Women and Post-Patriarchal Islam." In *After Patriarchy: Feminist Transformations of the World Religions*, ed. Paula M. Cooey, William R. Eakin, & Jay B. McDaniel. Maryknoll, NY: Orbis Books, 1991, 39–69.

Hoodfar, Homa. "The Veil in Their Minds and on Our Heads: Veiling Practices and Muslim Women." In *The Politics of Culture in the Shadow of Capital*, ed. and introd. Lowe, Lisa, & David Lloyd. Durham, NC: Duke University Press, 1997, 248-79.

Hopkins, Saleni. *Within the Purdah; Also, In the Zenana Homes of Indian Princess, and Heroes and Heroines of Zion; Being the Personal Observations of a Medical Missionary in India*. Cincinnati: Eaton and Mains, 1898.

Hosain, Attia (1953). *Phoenix Fled*. London: Virago, 1988.

Hosain, Attia (1961). *Sunlight on a Broken Column*. Delhi: Penguin Books, 1992.

Hossain, Hasina Yasmin. (1996). *Rokeya Sakhawat Hossain 1880-1932: The Status of Muslim Women in Bengal*. SOAS, University of London. (PhD thesis).

Hossain, Mary. "Women and Paradise." *Journal of European Studies*, 19 (1989), 293-310.

Houghton, R. C. *Women of the Orient: An Account of the Religious, Intellectual, Social Customs of the Women of Japan, China, India, and Turkey*. Cincinnati: Hitchcock and Walden, 1877.

Howland, Courtney W. (ed.). *Religious Fundamentalisms and the Human Rights of Women*. New York: St. Martin's Press, 1999.

Humphrey, Mrs. E. J. *Gems of India; or, Sketches of Distinguished Hindoo and Mohamedan Women*. New York: Nelson and Phillips, 1875.

Hussain, Iqbalunnisa. *Purdah and Polygamy: a life in an Indian Muslim household*. Bangalore: Hosali Press, 1944.

Ikramullah, Begum Shaista S. *From Purdah to Parliament*. London: The Crescent Press, 1963.

Inden, Ronald B. *Imagining India*. Oxford: Blackwell Publishers, 1990.

Iyengar, K.R. Srinivasa. *Indian Writings in English*. New Delhi: Sterling, 1983.

Jahan, (Nawab of Bhopal) Sultan. *Muslim Home*. Calcutta: Thacker, Spink & Co., 1916.

Jahan, Roushan (ed. & trans.). *Inside Seclusion: The Avarodhbasini of Rokeya Sakhawat Hossain*. Dhaka: Women for Women, 1981.

—— (ed. & trans.). *Sultana's Dream and selection from The Secluded Ones [by] Rokeya Sakhawat Hossain*. New York: The Feminist Press, 1988.

Jain, Jasbir. *Feminizing Political Discourse: Women and the Novel in India*. Jaipur: Rawat Publications, 1997.

—— (ed.). *Women's Writing: Text and Context*. Jaipur, Rawat, 1996.

—— (ed. & introd.); Amina Amin (ed.). *Margins of Erasure: Purdah in the Subcontinental Novel in English*. New Delhi: Sterling, 1995.

Jayawardena, Kumari. *The White Woman's Other Burden: Western Women and South Asia during British Colonial Rule*. New York: Routledge, 1995.

Jeffrey, Patricia. *Frogs in a well: Indian Women in Purdah*. London: Zed Books, 1979.

Jung, Anees. *Unveiling India: A Women's Journey.* New Delhi: Penguin Books, 1987.

Kabbani, Rana. *Europe's Myths of Orient: Devise and Rule*. London: Pandora Press, 1988.

Kafka, Phillipa. *On the Outside Looking In(dian): Indian Women Writers at Home and Abroad*. New York: Peter Lang, 2003.

Kahf, Mohja. "The Image of the Muslim Women in American Cinema: Two Orientalist Fantasy Films." *Cinefocus*, 3 (1995), 19–25.

——. *Western Representations of the Muslim Woman: From Termagant to Odalisque*. Austin, TX: University of Texas Press, 1999.

Kandiyoti, Deniz, (ed.). *Women, Islam and the State*. Temple University Press, 1991.

——."Islam and Feminism: A Misplaced Polarity." *WAF Journal*, 8 (1996), 10–13.

Karlekar, Malavika. *Voices from Within: Early Personal Narratives of Bengal Women*. Delhi: Oxford University Press, 1991.

Kaye, Jacqueline. "The Implications of a Too Regular Form: The Muslim Woman and the European Mind." In *Engendering Identities*, ed. and introd. Susan Castillo. Porto: Universidade Fernando Pessoa, 1996, 69-80.

Kazi, Seema. "Muslim Law and Women Living Under Muslim Laws." In *Muslim Women and the Politics of Participation: Implementing the Beijing Platform*, Ed. Mahnaz Afkhami, & Erika Friedl. Syracuse: Syracuse University Press, 1997, 141–146.

Kazmi, Syed Nasir Raza "E.M. Forester and Anita Desai: Portraits of Indian Muslims in English Fiction." In *English and Islam*, ed. J. U. Khan, & A. E. Hare. Kaula Lumpur, 1996, 161-174.

Khan, Maulana Wahiduddin. *Woman between Islam and Western Society*, trans. Farida Khanam. New Delhi: Al-Risala Books, 1995.

Khan, Mazhar-ul. *Purdah and Polygamy*. New Delhi: Harnam Publications, 1983.

Kidwai, A. R. *Orientalism in Lord Byron's "Turkish Tales"*. Lewiston: Mellen University Press, 1995.

——. "Oriental Heroines in Lord Byron's Turkish Tales", *Aligarh Journal of English Studies*, 20:1 (1998), 51-77.

—— (ed.). *Stranger Than Fiction: Images of Islam and Muslims in English Fiction*. India: APH Publishing Corporation, 2000.

King, J. S. *Islamic Feminism vs. Western Feminism: Analyzing a Conceptual Conflict*, 2003. Central Connecticut State University, Elihu Burritt Library Website: fred.ccsu.edu:8000/archive/00000056/01/etd-2003-11.pdf

Kothandarama Aiyar, K. S. *The Position of Women in India, in America, and Among Savages*. Madras: Gajapaty Press, 1897.

Kozlowski, Gregory C. "Muslim Women and the Control of Property in North India." *Indian Economic and Social History Review*, 24:2 (1987), 163-181.

Krishnan, E.V. Rama (ed.) *Indian Short Stories (1900-2000)*. Delhi: Sahitya Akademi, 2004.

Krishnamurthy, J. (ed). *Women in Colonial India: Essays on Survival, Work and the State*. Delhi: Oxford University Press, 1989.

Kumar, Amitava. *Husband of a Fanatic*. New Delhi: Penguin Books, 2004.

Kumar, Jainendra (tr. & ed.). *23 Hindi Short Stories*. New Delhi, Sahitya Akademy, 1998.

Kumar, Shiv K. *Contemporary Indian Short Stories in English.* Delhi: Sahitya Akademi, 1991.

_____. *Infatuation: The Crescent and Vermilion.* New Delhi, UBSPD, 2000.

Lateef, Shahida. *Muslim Women in India: Political and Private Realities 1890s—1980s.* New Delhi: Kali for Women, 1990.

Lemu, Aisha, & Fatima Heeren. *Women in Islam.* Leister: Islamic Foundation, 1976.

Lewis, Reina. *Gendering Orientalism: Race, Femininity, and Representation.* London: Routledge, 1996.

Liddle, Joanna, & Rama Joshi. "Gender and Imperialism in British India," *Economic and Political Weekly*, 20(43) (1985).

Luther, Rauf (trans.). *Truth unveiled: translation of Mussaddas-e Hali.* Lahore: Sh. Mubarak Ali, 1978.

McClintock, Anne. *Imperial Leather: Race, Gender and Sexuality in the Colonial Contest.* London, New York: Routledge, 1995.

McLoughlin, Seán. "An Underclass in Purdah: Discrepant Representations of Identity and the Experiences of Young-British-Asian-Muslim-Women." *Bulletin of the John Rylands University Library of Manchester*, 80:3 (1998), 89-106.

Macmillan, Margaret. *Women of the Raj.* New York: Thames and Hudson, 1988.

Madhavananda, Swami, & R. C. Majumdar (eds.). *Great Women of India.* Almora: Advaita Ashrama, 1982.

Mahmud, Mushfeqa. *Patre Rokeya Parichiti* [Rokeya in letters]. Dhaka: Bangla Academy, 1965.

Mahmud, Shamsun Nahar. *Rokeya Jibani* [Life of Rokeya]. Calcutta: Bulbul Publishing House, 1937.

Malak, Amin. *Muslim Narratives and the Discourse of English*. New York: State University of New York Press, 2005.

Marková, Dagmar. "Hindu and Muslim Women in the Light of the Respective Orthodox Popular Educational Booklets." *Archív Orientální: Quarterly Journal of African and Asian Studies*, 72:4 (2004), 454-75.

Matar, Nabil. "Muslim and Non-Muslim Women in the Empires of Islam, 1453-1798." *The Muslim World*, 95:2 (2005), 165-223.

Maududi, Sayyid Abul A'la. *Purdah and the Status of Women in Islam*. Delhi: Markazi Maktaba Islami, 1994.

Melman, Billie. *Women's Orients: English Women and the Middle East, 1718-1918: Sexuality, Religion and Work*. London: Macmillan, 1992.

Mehrotra, Deepti Priya. *Home Truths: Stories of Single Mothers*. New Delhi: Penguin Books, 2003.

Memon, Muhammad Umar (ed.) *An Epic Unwritten: The Penguin Book of Partition Stories from Urdu*. New Delhi: Penguin Books, 1998.

Mernissi, Fatima. *Beyond the Veil: Male-Female Dynamics in Modern Muslim Society*. Bloomington, IN: Indiana University Press, 1990.

Mesbah, Muhammad Taqi, Muhammad Jawad Bahonar, & Lois Lamya al-Faruqi. *Status of Women in Islam*. New Delhi: Radiant, 1990.

Metcalf, Barbara D. (1994). "Reading and Writing about Muslim Women in British India." In *Forging Identities: Gender, Communities And the State*, ed. Zoya Hasan. Delhi: Kali for Women, 1994, 1-22.

_____. *Perfecting Women, Maulana Ashraf Ali Thanawi's Bihishti Zewar*. Delhi: Oxford University Press, 1992.

_____. (ed) *Moral Conduct and Moral Authority: Tha Place of Adab in South Asian Islam*. Berkeley: University of California Press, 1984.

_____. *Islamic Reform and Islamic Women: Maulana Thanawi's Jewelry of Paradise in Moral Conduct and Authority*. Berkeley, 1984

Mahindra, Indra. *The Club*. New Delhi: UBSPD, 1984.

Mies, Maria. *Indian Women and Patriarchy*. Delhi: Concept, 1980.

Minault, Gail. *Women and Political Participation in India and Pakistan*. Columbia, MO, South Asia Books, 1982.

_____. "Purdah's Progress: The Beginnings of School Education for Indian Muslim Women." In *Individuals and Ideas in Modern India*, ed. Jagdish P. Sharma. Calcutta: Firma KLM, 1982, 76-97.

_____. "Hali's *Majalis un Nisa*: Purdah and Woman Power in Nineteenth Century India." In *Islamic Society and Culture*, ed. M. Israel, & N. K. Wagle. Delhi: Manohar, 1983, 39-49.

_____. "Shaikh Abdullah, Begum Abdullah and Sharif Education for Girls at Aligarh." In *Modernization and Social Change among Muslims in India*, ed. Imtiaz Ahmad. New Delhi: Manohar, 1983, 207-36.

_____. "Making Invisible Women Visible: Studying the History of Muslim Women in South Asia." *Journal of South Asian Studies*, 9:1 (1986), 1-14.

_____. (trans. ed.). *Voices of Silence: English translation of Khwaja Altaf Hussain Hali's Majalis un-nissa and Chup ke dad*. Delhi: Chanakya Publications, 1986.

_____. "Sayyid Mumtaz Ali and 'Huquq un-Niswan': An Advocate of Women's Rights in Islam in the Late Nineteenth Century." *Modern Asian Studies*, 24:1 (1990), 147-72.

_____. "*Ismat*: Rashid ul Khairi's novels and Urdu literary journalism for women." In *Urdu and Muslim South Asia*, ed. Christopher Shackle. Delhi: Oxford University Press, 1991.

_____. "Sayyed Mumtaz Ali and *Tehzib-un-Niswan*: Women's Rights in Islam and Women's Journalism in Urdu." In *Religious Controversy in British India: Dialogues in South Asian Languages*, ed. Kenneth W. Jones. Albany: State University of New York Press, 1992, 179-99.

_____. "Other Voices, Other Rooms: The View from the Zenana." In *Women as Subjects: South Asian Histories*, ed. Nita Kumar. Charlottesville, VA: University Press of Virginia, 1994, 108-124.

_____. *Secluded Scholars: Women's Education and Muslim Social Reform in Colonial India*. Delhi: Oxford University Press, 1998.

Mirza, Sarfazar Hussain. *Muslim Women's Role in the Pakistan Movement*. Lahore: Research Society of Pakistan, 1969.

Misra, Rekha. *Women in Mughal India*. Delhi: Munshiram Manoharlal, 1967.

Moghadam, Valentine M. *Gender and National Identity: Women and Politics in Muslim Society*. Karachi: Oxford University Press, 1994.

_____. "Islamic Feminism and Its Discontents: Toward a Resolution of the Debate." *Signs*, 27:4 (2002), 1135-71.

Moghissi, Haideh. *Feminism and Islamic Fundamentalism, The Limits of Postmodern Analysis*. London: Zed Press, 1999.

Mohamad, Maznah. "Poststructuralism, Power and Third World Feminism." *Kajian Malaysia*, 12:1–2 (1994), 119–143.

Mohammad, Robina. "Marginalisation, Islamism and the Production of the 'Other's 'Other'." *Gender, Place and Culture: A Journal of Feminist Geography*, 6:3 (1999), 221–241.

Mohanty, Chandra Talpade. "Under Western Eyes: Feminist Scholarship and Colonial Discourses" (1986). In *Colonial Discourse and Post-Colonial Theory: A Reader*, ed. Patrick Williams, & Laura Chrisman. London, Harvester Wheatsheaf, 1993, 196-220.

_____, Ann Russo, & Lourdes Torres. *Third World Women and the Politics of Feminism*. Bloomington: Indiana University Press, 1991.

Mojab, Shahrzad. "'Muslim' Women and 'Western' Feminists: the debate on Particulars and Universals." *Monthly Review: An Independent Socialist Magazine*, 50:7 (1998), 19–31.

——. "Theorizing the Politics of 'Islamic Feminism'." *Feminist Review*, 69 (Winter 2001), 124–146.

Mumtaz, Khawar, & Farida Shaheed. *Women of Pakistan: Two Steps Forward, One Step Back?*. London: Zed Books, 1987.

Murshid, Ghulam. (1983). *Reluctant Debutante: Response of Bengali Women to Modernization, 1849-1905*. Rajshahi University, Bangladesh: Sahitya Samsad, 1983.

Naim, C.M. (Ed.) *Quratulain Hyder's A Season of Betrayals: A Short Story and Two Novellas.* New Delhi: Kali for Women, 1999.

Nancoo, Lynda. "Marriage-able? Cultural Perspectives of Women with Disabilities of South Asian Origin." *Canadian Woman Studies*, 13:4 (1993), 49–51.

Nanda, B. R. (ed.). *Indian Women: From Purdah to Modernity*. New Delhi: Nehru Memorial Library and Radiant Pub., 1990.

Okin, Susan Moller (ed.) *Is Multiculturalism Bad for Women*? Princeton: Princeton University Press, 1999.

Pandurang, Mala. "Conceptualizing Emigrant Indian Female Subjectivity: Possible Entry Points." In *South Asian Women in the Diaspora*, ed. Nirmal Puwar, & Parvati Raghuram. New York: Berg, 2003, 87–95.

Papanek, Hanna. "Purdah: Separate Worlds and Symbolic Shelter." *Comparative Studies in Society and History*, 15:3 (1973), 289-325.

——, & Gail Minault (ed.). *Separate Worlds: Studies of Purdah in South Asia*. New Delhi: Chanakya Publications, 1982.

——. "Caging the Lion: A Fable for Our Time." In *Sultana's Dream and selection from The Secluded Ones [by] Rokeya Sakhawat Hossain*, ed. Roushan Jahan. The City University of New York: The Feminist Press, 1988, 58-85.

Parks, F. *Wanderings of a Pilgrim in Search of the Picturesque during four-and-twenty years in the East with Revelations of Life in Zenana* Vol. 1. London: Pelham Richardson, 1850.

Pool, John J. *Woman's Influence in the East: As Shown in the Noble Lives of Past Queens and Princess of India*. London: E. F. Stock, 1892.

Qureshi, Regula B. "Marriage Strategies among Muslims from South Asia." In *Muslim Families in North America*, ed. Earle H. Waugh, Sharon M. Abu-Laban, & Regula Qureshi. Edmonton: University of Alberta Press, 1991, 185–212.

Rahman, Tabassum A. "The Experiences of South Asian American Muslim Women: A Postmodern Approach." Alliant International University, 2003 (Ph.D. thesis).

Report of the Committee appointed by the Govt to consider the question of legislative interference for preventing the excessive abuse of polygamy. Calcutta: B. S. Press 1867.

Report Ijlas-e Awwal: Muslim Ladies Conference, Aligarh, March 1914. Aligarh: Dar Mutabeh Institute, 1915.

Ravikant, & Tarun K. Saint (eds.) *Translating Partition*. New Delhi: Katha Books, 2001.

Ray, Bharati. *Early Feminists of Colonial India: Sarala Devi Chaudhurani and Rokeya Sakhawat Hossain*. Delhi: Oxford University Press, 2002.

Richardson, Alan. "Romanticism and the Colonization of the Feminine." In *Romanticism and Feminism*. ed. Anne K. Mellor. Bloomington: Indiana University Press, 1988.

Rokeya, B. (1904). *Motichur-I*. In *Rokeya Rachanabali* (2nd ed.), ed. Abdul Quadir. Dhaka: Bangla Academy, 1999, 1-54.

Rokeya, B. (1905). *Sultana's Dream*. In *Rokeya Rachanabali* (2nd ed.), ed. Abdul Quadir. Dhaka: Bangla Academy, 1999, 461-474.

Rokeya, B. (1922). *Motichur-II*. In *Rokeya Rachanabali* (2nd ed.), ed.Abdul Quadir. Dhaka: Bangla Academy, 1999, 55-182.

Rokeya, B. (1924). *Padmaraga*. In *Rokeya Rachanabali* (2nd ed.), ed.Abdul Quadir. Dhaka: Bangla Academy, 1999, 255-368.

Rokeya, B. (1927). "God Gives, Man Robs." In *Rokeya Rachanabali* (2nd ed.), ed.Abdul Quadir. Dhaka: Bangla Academy, 1999, 477-478.

Rokeya, B. (1931). *Aborodhbasini*. In *Rokeya Rachanabali* (2nd ed.), ed. Abdul Quadir. Dhaka: Bangla Academy, 1999, 371-405.

Sahgal, Nayantara. *Mistaken Identity*. London, Heinemann, 1988.

Said, E. W. *Orientalism: Western Conceptions of the Orient*. London: Penguin Books, 1978

——. *Culture and Imperialism*. London: Vintage, 1994.

Saifullah-Khan, Verity. "Asian Women in Britain: Strategies of Adjustment of Indian and Pakistani Migrants." *Social Action*, 25:3 (1975), 302–330.

——. "Pakistani Women in Britain." *New Community*, 5:1–2 (1976), 99–108.

——. "Purdah in the British Situation." In *Dependence and Exploitation in Work and Marriage,* ed. Diana L. Barker, & Sheila Allen. London: Longman, 1976, 224–245.

Saleh, Fatma. *A New Perspective: Women in Islam*. Costa Mesa, CA: The Islamic Educational Center of Orange County, 2001.

Sangari, Kumkum, & Sudesh Vaid (ed.). *Recasting Women: Essays in Colonial History*. New Delhi: Kali for Women, 1989.

Sarker, Sonita. "Larger Than Bengal: Feminism in Rokeya Sakhawat Hossain's *Sultana's Dream* and Global Modernities." *Archiv orientalni: Quarterly Journal of Asian and African Studies*, (2000), 441-456.

Satthianadhan, Anna. *A Brief Account of Zenana Work in Madras*. London: Seeley, 1878.

Saiyid, Dushka Hyder. *Muslim Women of the British Punjab: From Seclusion to Politics*. New York: St. Martin's Press. 1998.

Settar, S.& Indira Baptista Gupta (eds.) *Pangs of Partition: The Parting of Ways.* 2 Vols. New Delhi: Manohar Publishers, 2002.

Shamsie, M. Attia Hosain (1913-1998). The Literary Encyclopedia, 2004. http://www.litencyc.com/php/speople.php?rec=true&UID=2216

Sharpe, Jenny. *Allegories of Empire: The Figure of the Woman in the Colonial Text*. Minneapolis: University of Minnesota Press, 1993.

Shirazi, Faegheh. *The Veil Unveiled: The Hijab in Modern Culture*. Gainesville: University Press of Florida, 2001.

Showeb, M. "The Position of Indian Muslim Women in Changing Social Structure of Islam." *New Quest*, 85 (Jan-Feb 1991), 41-43.

Shuraydi, Muhammad, & Arshia U. Zaidi. "Perceptions of Arranged Marriages by Young Pakistani Muslim Women Living in a

Western Society." *Journal of Comparative Family Studies*, 33:4 (2002), 37–57.

Singh, Khushwant. *The Company of Women*. New Delhi: Viking, 1999.

———. *Delhi*. Delhi: Penguin Books, 1990.

Sonbol, Amira (ed.). *Women, Family Law and Divorce in Islamic Society*, Styracuse: Syracuse University Press, 1996.

Sorabji, Cornelia. *Love and Life Behind the Purdah*. London: Freemantle, 1901.

Spivak, Gayatri C. "Three Women's Texts and a Critique of Imperialism." In C. Belsey & J. Moore (Ed.), *The Feminist Reader: Essays in Gender and the Politics of Literary Criticism*. London: Macmillan, 1997, 148-163.

———. "Three Women's Texts and a Critique of Imperialism." *Critical Inquiry*, 12 (1985): 242-61.

Stacey, Aisha Tahira (2005). "Women in Islam: Oppression or Liberation?" http://islamonline.net/English/family/2005/03/article01.shtml

Suleri, Sara. *The Rhetoric of English India*. Chicago: University of Chicago Press, 1992.

Storrow, Edward. *Our Indian Sisters*. London: Religious Tract Society, 1898.

Stowasser, Barbara Freyer. "The Hijab: How a Curtain Became an Institution and a Cultural Symbol." In *Humanism, Culture, and Language in the Near East: Studies in Honor of Georg Krotkoff*, eds. Asma Afsaruddin, & A. H. Mathias Zahniser. Winona Lake, IN: Eisenbrauns, 1997, 87-104.

Sultaan, Abida. "The Begums of Bhopal." *History Today* 30 (Oct. 1980), 30-35.

Sunder Rajan, Rajeswari. *Real and Imagined Women: Gender, culture and postcolonialism*. London: Routledge, 1993.

Swart, Susanna Maria. *Beyond the Veil: Muslim Women Write Back.* University of Pretoria, 2000. (dissertation)

Takhar, Shaminder. "South Asian Women and the Question of Political Organization." In *South Asian Women in the Diaspora*, ed. Nirmal Puwar, & Parvati Raghuram. New York: Berg, 2003, 215–226.

Taj, pseud. *Zorah: a tale of zenana life*. London: Methuen, 1912

Thanawi, Ashraf Ali. *Bahishti Zewar or Heavenly Ornament*, trans. Farid Uddin. Delhi: Taj Company, 1983.

Tharu, Susie, & K. Lalita (ed.). *Women Writing in India: 600 BC to the Present* (in two volumes). Delhi: Oxford University Press, 1991-93.

Thobani, Sunera. "Making the Links: South Asian Women and the Struggle for Reproductive Rights." *Canadian Woman Studies*, 13:1 (1992), 19–22.

Trumpener, Katie. "Rewriting Roxane: Orientalism and Intertextuality in Montesquieus's *Letters Persanes* and Defoe's *The Fortunate Mistress*." *Stanford French Review*, 11 (1987),177-191.

Urquhart, M. M. *Women in Bengal*. London: Y. M. C. A., 1925.

Vatuk, Sylvia. "*Hamara Daur-i Hayat*: An Indian Muslim Woman Writes Her Life." In *Telling Lives in India: Biography, Autobiography, and Life History*, ed. and introd. David Arnold, & Stuart Blackburn. Bloomington, IN: Indiana University Press, 2004, 144-74.

Visram, Rozina. *Women in India and Pakistan: The struggle for Independence from British rule*. Cambridge: Cambridge University Press, 1992.

Wadud, Amina. "Woman and Islam: Beyond the Stereotypes." *Pakistan Journal of Women's Studies: Alam-e-Niswan*, 4:2 (1997), 1–14.

——. "A'ishah's Legacy." *New Internationalist*, 345 (May 2002): 16–17.

——. "Alternative Qur'anic Interpretation and the Status of Muslim Women." In *Windows of Faith: Muslim Women Scholar-Activists*, ed. Gisela Webb. New York: Syracuse University Press, 2000, 3-21.

——. *Qur'an and Woman: Rereading the Sacred Text from a Woman's Perspective*. 2d ed. New York: Oxford University Press, 1999.

Warren, F.M. "The Enamoured Moslem Princess in Orderic Vital and the French Epic", *PMLA*, 29 (1914), 341-358.

Wann, Louis. "The Oriental in Elizabethan Drama." *Modern Philology*, 12:7 (1915), 423-47.

Women of South Asian Descent Collective (ed.). *Our Feet Walk the Sky: Women of the South Asian Diaspora*. San Francisco: Aunt Lute Books, 1993.

Yamani, Mai (ed.). *Feminism and Islam: Legal and Literary Perspectives*. Reading: Ithaca Press, 1996.

——, & Andrew Allen (eds.). *Feminism and Islam: Legal and Literary Perspectives*. New York: New York University Press, 1996.

Yeazell, Ruth Bernard. *Harems of the Mind: Passages of Western Art and Literature*. New Haven: Yale University Press, 2000.

Yegenoglu, Meyda. *Colonial Fantasies: Towards a Feminist Reading of Orientalism*. Cambridge: Cambridge University Press, 1998.

Yuval-Davis, Nira. "Fundamentalism, Multiculturalism and Women in Britain." In *'Race', Culture and Difference*, ed. James Donald, & Ali Rattansi. London: Sage Publications, 1992, 278–291.

Zafar, Fareeha (ed). *Finding Our Way : Readings on Women in Pakistan*. Lahore: ASR, 1991.

Zaiba, Shujah Ahmad. *Maulvi Nazir Ahmad and Aligarh Tahrik* [Maulvi Nazir Ahmad and Aligarh Movement]; Karachi: Maktabah Aslub, 1987.

Zaidi, S. M. H. *Position of Women under Islam*. Calcutta: Book Tower, 1932

Zaman, Niaz *A Divided Legacy: The Partition in Selected Novels of India, Pakistan and Bangladesh*. Karachi: Oxford University Press, 2001.

Index